TRUSTING GOD'S PROCESS

AS YOU GO THROUGH

Garry Washington

Edited by K. Lee

KLEPub.com

All rights reserved. No part of this book may be reproduced or transmitted in any form or by any means, electronic or mechanical, including photocopying, recording or any information storage and retrieval system without written permission of the publisher except for brief quotations used in reviews, written specifically for inclusion in a newspaper, blog, magazine, or academic paper.

Self Publishing services provided by Krystal Lee Enterprises (KLE Publishing) Copyright © 2022 by Devotis Lee. All rights reserved. Edited by K. Lee

Please send comments and questions:
Garry Washington
Website: GarryWashington.com
GWSpeaks.com
Garry@KLEPub.com

Krystal Lee Enterprises LLC
www.KLEPub.com   770-240-0089 Ext. 1
services@klepub.com or sales@klepub.com
IG,FB: @KLEPUB

Printed in the United States of America.

ISBN: 978-1-945066-14-6

Dedication

There are three outstanding persons' that, if it weren't for them, I wouldn't be who I am or still becoming…

The First:
    My Heavenly Father, my LORD & Savior, my friend, my provider, my counselor, my DADDY, my GOD. He is JESUS CHRIST, the KING OF ETERNITY. I'm so truly grateful to Him for absolutely everything that has been done, that will be done, & for what He's doing right now. My heart is "swelling up" with unexplainable words as I'm expressing my love, my adoration, and appreciation for His heart towards me.

Second:
    My awesome wife who is a true, humble, & great woman Of God, Shirley (Shirl). She has been there during my spiritual growth journey. Praying with & for me every night. Walking beside me through my fight to live holy from day 1 of us meeting. She's not only my wife but my partner and my friend. Yeah, we worship together, we love 2getha, and we enjoy one another's company. Shirl, I truly bless The LORD for you every day, and I humbly thank Him for your heart towards me.
    Luv U 2 Life!!

Third:
    My daughter, Shanice, Lilmomma, You are a light to my heart. A true spirit whose heart & intent is to be a blessing to others. This is who you are to me ALWAYS. I love you more than you really know…

Acknowledgments

Krystal, my dear sister. The LORD had arranged for our meeting, to grow as 'family' to bring Glory & Honor to Him. Dr. Lee has been more than just my sista, her very intention is to avidly advocate The Father, in the way she addresses Him and how she interacts with me. I listen to her heart when she's talking with her children, talking about someone or something. Krystal, I love You, my sista & you can't do nothing about it.

Kino, my heartfelt love & appreciation for you & your great family is an honor & privilege to sit, laugh, eat, hang out, talk Jesus, and talk about any and everything with you. The LORD is WONDERFUL in that He allowed our paths to meet & connect with love, respect & appreciation for Him and for one another. To God Be ALL THE GLORY!!

To Dr. Jerome & Lady Marsha Stokes, I want to humbly thank y'all from the bottom of my heart. You both so humbly allow our Great LORD and Master to use y'all to instruct others and to live a life that represents how a true man & woman of God ought to walk. I'm humbly honored to be able to sit under a "general-in-holiness" who isn't afraid to speak "thus saith The LORD!" Pastor and Sis. Marsha, I love y'all, thank you!!

Elder. James Patterson. You are my cousin, but you are also a mighty man of God that has poured so much into me. I thank you, truly!!! The LORD had placed you in my life, in my heart for His Glory and my benefit. Cuz, you have taken me under your "wing" & shown me, by instructing me to have "a true relationship with God." I believe you were instructed by The Holy Spirit to show me how to grow to be in love with The LORD. I learned how to conduct myself as a "representative of holiness" & sooooo many other things because of you!! Cuz, I'm starting to cry, over here. I'll just say this from my heart, I LOVE YOU...

Dr. David Daniels, 'Rev', thank you Man of God for being my friend when I was new in Christ and even up until now. You are a "blessing to The Body of Christ". You ALWAYS had my back, and always showed me the 'holy' steps to take for spiritual growth. You & Sis Velma's heart towards Shirl & I is 'branded' in heaven & in Shirl & my heart forever. Love you, Rev...

Eld. Jeffery Sams, 'Doc', I want to thank you for pushing me to pursue this project. Our "mountain" journeys' were truly "the cherry on top of the cake." Jeff, you & Sis. Annette are more than "warriors." Shirl & I luv y'all 2 life...

Eld. Lloyd Curtis, Man of God, you have been there for me when I didn't know what was going on. The LORD had placed you as " the brother who is there in a time of need." I'm truly grateful for you loving on me as your brother, 4real. Bruh, it's a privilege & an honor to be your brother and your friend. Thank you!!!

Eld. Steve Harris, (Lil Apostle) lol. Thank you for Always encouraging me. The LORD always had you to say the right things to me to keep me encouraged. Thank you for your time and your genuine personality. I love You with no take-backs.

Table Of Contents

Introduction...9

Each of Us Have a Battle...15

Scripture is the Foundation of Our Faith...25

He Has a Purpose for Your Life...37

Coming to Know Him...47

Growing Your Relationship with God...59

Obeying His Commands ...67

Keep Your Eyes on Heavenly Things...79

Renew Your Mind...89

Persevere and Never Turn Back!...99

The Penalty of Doing Things Your Way...109

A Conclusion on The Matter...123

About The Author...137

KLE Details...138

Introduction

Everything we do in life has a process. There are steps involved in any victory. For life, we have a process that God takes us through and we trust that this journey will make us more like Him our Father, whom I call Daddy. You see God is personal to me and I believe He takes us through a process and not over challenges, problems, and struggles so that we learn His character and goodness intimately. This book is dedicated to trusting the process that you will have to endure–and you can because you are not alone. Daddy is with you and He will never leave nor forsake you is His promise to us.

WOW!!!

When I thought of writing this book, I didn't expect this. I mean, I was so 'gun-ho' about this project. I have been preaching and teaching for years and I have longed for a time to write and publish a book! The LORD has been giving me all kinds of messages that I could use for this project. He has absolutely blessed me with two God-fearing, Holy Ghost-filled, lovers of Himself, Dr. Krystal Lee & Kino Glover that have been directing me. At times, they both have encouraged me to follow The Spirit and let Him show me the right way to travel with this assignment.

Also, The LORD has given me a tremendous woman of God. My wonderful wife Shirley (Shirl) to be by my side who is always loving on me. She encourages me to go & pursue what The LORD will have me to do and I appreciate her for that always.

I'm too happy about doing this right now! I should be ready to write as this project has been pending for a year–almost two years now. I know that I must trust The LORD to open my heart & mind to perceive what He wants to download to me. Then I need Him to keep my fingers good to type and my back strong to keep the posture. And all this, to ensure I can release this powerful word of encouragement to you my 'brothas and sistas.' Let's see what happens next!

My mind goes blank when I sit at this computer. Funny, because I had a message just in my mind with a working title a moment ago. Then all of a sudden, I can't hear nothing! It's like I see white space or the plug has been pulled from the tv and you see black covering the screen. No voices, no people, no images, and no sounds. Nothing! This should not be so.

The Spirit of God speaks to me and I hear Him the same way I can hear you. This wasn't an instantaneous thing but a process, a relationship had to be built. I trust this Voice and right now I am struggling. My back is starting to ache, my fingers are beginning to cramp, and the passion for this project is quickly dimming. It's as if my passion to write this book has run away from my heart!

All of a sudden, soooooo many other things start to come up that are trying to draw my attention and love away from this project. These distractions are attempting to refocus my passion and intent on writing what I had just decided–after much debate to write! "LORD," I began to pray, "what is it that I'm supposed to say? How are You Oh LORD, going to direct your servant to encourage your children?" Trusting God's Process As You're Going Through, wasn't the working title or subject in my mind until after I prayed–again!

You see family, my heart wanted to speak on coming from a place where I didn't know the true & living God and then getting to know Him. 'Growing to Have a Relationship with The LORD, On His Terms" was the title I had thought to work with. Too many options can be just as overwhelming as not having anything sometimes. But DADDY, (that's what I call Him), enacted His will and cleared my mind just like that! His will is what I seek to do, so I'm cool with the change. So, for those hearts that are still seeking The LORD, still holding onto His promises, The LORD has something GREAT in store for you!

First, JESUS HIMSELF said this to the ones that are still holding on. "But he that shall endure unto the end, the same shall be saved" (Matt 24:13). Endure, enduring what any sane person would ask? You mean to tell me, you and I have to endure the crazy–don't make no sense moments happening in our lives? I know you think like I do, I didn't create this foolishness that's happening in my life.

Why do we have to endure things we didn't

choose? How are we supposed to be normal when the shaking that's taken place is shifting the floor out from under us? Endure, no matter how much I'm suffering? If you're like me you would say, "You want me to tolerate all kinds of foolishness and do this without giving up?"

Father this world ain't easy and many of your soldiers out here battling. It's a whole lot of enduring we go through in a lifetime especially if you come from where I've been. Only then will 'I be saved' I ask myself and trust you do too! I am to keep the faith and not give out, no matter the pressure on me?

LORD, I thought you already saved me from hell when I went to the altar or said a prayer some may think. Some think because they got a dedication paper or a fuzzy feeling in their heart, they're good. But according to your word, "According as He has chosen us in Him before the foundation of the world, that we should be holy and without blame before Him in love" (Eph 1:4).

Yes!!! This is for the hearts that are still holding onto God's promises. Endure, endurance, is this part of God's process you ponder? I am going to tell you like this, look at this world before the global pandemic. The years were 2020 to 2022 roughly when the world seemed to shut down overnight. We were all trying to get through what we thought or heard had occurred. The fear put an abrupt stop to our day-to-day lives, and for some, it was the cause for their break in relationship with God due to a lack of fellowship.

Since then, folks have gotten extremely aggressive with "life." Some are trying to "make up for lost time," which is impossible to do. Only the Father can redeem the time we lose (Ephesians 5:16). Some of us have spent the time doing much of nothing for God.

Believers at one time were preaching it was the end of the world because we had fallen into the trap of the world. The church started talking out of the same fear the world had and those teachings were going unchecked. True, we have been in the last days since Christ left, but No Man knows the hour of His return– But! He is coming back!

Anyway, folks are in "hot pursuit" of anything and everything that's a priority to their hearts. Survival has always been important to men's and women's hearts. No one has to teach you to self-preserve, it is a built-in system. If someone asked you to hold your breath until you died, you could only do it for so long, before your mouth will be forced open by your inner self to breathe.

Family, this is a fact, God's ways are not our ways! And our inner self is not in subjection to His authority because of the fall of man, and the rebellious spirit or nature we all possess at birth! Micah 4:2 (b) says of God, "And He will teach us His ways and we will walk in His paths."

So, since we don't know what The True God knows, who has created ALL THINGS (you & I included), who else is best to know what is good for us? His process works. I'm a living witness of it. I can say it with a solemn conviction, so Imma (I will for the professional English speakers) say it with a solemn conviction ást# GOD'S PROCESS WORKS!!

Each of Us Have a Battle

The "struggle" is real for every breathing soul because we all have something we are battling. There cannot be a war if there is no fight, no confrontation, or two sides warring for a victory. This war can be a battle you are fighting emotionally, financially, mentally, physically, or spiritually and this or these confrontations will cause friction in a person's life.

Each of us has a "battle" and many of us have a multilayered battle that we are fighting. It is not just an emotional war for some of us, it is also a financial war. If our finances are good, it seems like we are fighting mentally to maintain. If the battle is spiritual, it seems like a physical attack jumps in with mental anguish tied at the hip!

When we undergo an attack in our lives, this pressure can weigh on us and at times causes us to become weak. Not that we're powerless but we are made to see the limits of our jobs, our minds, and our bodies. We are not all-powerful and able to bear all things unless we have the power of God working through us. His power is what sustains us in our weakness. You see, in our weakness, God is made strong (2 Corinthians 12:9)!

What happens if we don't have His power, His Spirit, working within us? This pressure can cause us to fall victim to dangerous thoughts or actions. We can, & do at times, become heavy and overwhelmed by those feelings and that pressure can feel unbearable. Can you relate to having a battle that seemed to knock the wind out of you at impact?

Maybe you were making plans to go to school, and a family member goes to jail and you feel obligated to help them out? Or maybe you have plans to leave town, and your mom or dad falls sick, so you feel obligated to stay? Maybe you made arrangements to take a vacation and your job demands that you stay or face losing your job? These hard decisions you and I have to make, the feeling, the weight, can make us feel lost. This discouraging feeling can make us think crazy thoughts and even take rash actions.

Many of us have made choices I know we have lived on to regret. Or is it just me that has made some choices that I know I shouldn't have? I chose to live a life I wasn't raised to live. I accepted friendships that I knew would be a problem. I ignored my Momma when she said, "Leave them alone. Stop going over there." Like you may have heard, I went anyway.

I snuck out of the house to run the streets and hang out with who I thought were my friends. I chased women that looked good on the outside without a care for what they had going on, on the inside. I allowed my flesh to run amock because I was all about fulfilling my desires. I was me-focused and I didn't care nothing about nobody deep down, although I told myself I did.

It's funny how we can look at what we were, and celebrate where we are today. But we struggle something strong to see where we are and believe for where we are going! There are times we are fighting the good fight and the enemy can have us feel like, 'I can't do this no more.' We think, 'Wait a minute, I can duck out of this madness. I can escape this part of the process.'

We keep talking and say, 'I'm not gonna fight this, forget this foolishness, this pressure is too much!' Some give up, some say, 'It ain't worth me losing my mind over this.' Now, in going through all of this, why would I believe–let alone 'trust' any process, including God's process, if that means I gotta go through sooooo much to prove I love Him? I mean doesn't He know that already?

He pulled me out of my mess. He rescued many of us from drugs, addictions, silly men, or silly women. He stopped us from the old man and birthed us into a new man. He made me a new creature but now I am still fighting? I thought after my conversion I would have sunny days ahead and no worries. Why am I having trouble on every side? I am not a sinner no more. I am a child of God! So why do I feel like the gates of hell are coming against me?

He said in His Word, that He knows everything, so don't He know that I love Him? Isn't He the one that's allowing me to suffer? "My momma died & she was a good woman," some may say. "I got laid off & I got these children to feed," some may say. "These bills are cramping my chest." "My daughter is losing her mind & my son lost his mind," some may say. "My neighbors are foul, my attitude truthfully isn't good," some may say. "I know I'm supposed to hold on but holding on ain't helping," some may say! These are the words from those that claim they love Jesus may I point out. Those who say they believe Him for salvation and heaven, but can't endure the common things of earth!

    I remember one afternoon deciding to go see my mother. It was a somber day and I was not my best self. I was running from some things internally because I never backed down from a man or a woman. It was not in me to be a coward. I knew seeing my mother would be heart-wrenching because I didn't want her to see me less than my best.

    I always looked good and had my own style, I will later explain more, but on this day I was wearing jean shorts, a collared shirt, white shoes, and sporting red hair. Can you imagine, a chocolate brother like myself was born with red hair like my mother? Now, my hair is more peppered black and white today than red, but I had a Malcolm X vibe for a minute in my younger days.

    So my sister agreed to let me and the woman I was seeing at the time catch a ride with her. My mother never approved of her and I was glad she sat in the lobby when I went in to talk to her. Sometimes you don't know why things happen when you are going through, but when you look back, you understand. The drive to the hospital was silent. I tried everything to distract my heart from feeling the grip it was enduring.

I wished that this day had not come because I just didn't feel comfortable about it. It was like the air, the sky, and everything knew something that I was going to find out. I looked out the window searching for something, but I didn't know what to find. Have you ever had a longing for something that you could not put into words? Something you wanted to see or feel, that seemed to never come?

So we pull up to the hospital and enter the building. It would appear we were the last of my siblings to arrive. They were waiting for us in a smaller lobby down from her door. As we all greeted each other and exchanged words of quick encouragement they all turned to head for her room. Then all of sudden, my feet turned to cement. I couldn't move, I couldn't go where they were going. I don't know if it was fear, guilt, shame, or just an uneasy feeling–but I knew I couldn't shake it.

My family headed into the room and I awaited their reappearance back. I was so wrapped up in my feelings and thoughts, I didn't realize if my girl went into the room or not. Truthfully, I didn't care. They all tried to get me to go into the room, but I couldn't bring myself to do it. I couldn't face her.

My mother and I were cool my entire upbringing. We had a connection that was all our own. My mother had four children and she treated us all differently. I have an older sister, the only girl my mom had. I am the oldest son, and then I have two brothers underneath me. We were all unique in my mother's eyes.

My sister because she was the only girl. I was the oldest son, my younger brother battled sickness growing up, and my youngest brother was the baby. My mom treated us all differently and she didn't care about how anyone felt. Funny, we all understood it. No one felt like they weren't important or precious to her. We all knew she loved us all she just gave us what we individually needed.

She was a great example of what love is and how it works. Love is an action and love in action will help you to grow talents you never thought were yours. My mom was a practicing nurse at our home. No matter what happened to you, my mother could work out a miracle. She was the kind of mother to work up a concoction like Jesus and take spit and water and work it out!

She gave us all confidence, hope, and encouraged us to be our very best selves. I remember she told me growing up, "No matter what you decided to do or become, be the best! If you want to be a doctor, lawyer, or businessman be the best. If you want to be a bum be the best at that. But never let someone best you at being your best self."

I never forgot her words and I never will. I always wanted to make her smile and be proud of me. She never voiced how she felt about everything I had done, she respected my choices even if she didn't agree. I loved that her love for me never changed and she loved me unconditionally when I needed it in every phase of my life while she was alive.

My mother was a good woman and I am grateful to the Father for her. As my family exited the room, they told me she wanted to see me. I just had this feeling that I couldn't leave without seeing her. I wanted support at that moment, but I knew I had to walk in alone, so I did. My mother was a Jehovah's Witness, so she had strong convictions. I loved that part about her, and that she was never a punk even when being a saint!

I came into the room and I saw her sitting at the edge of the bed. She was looking toward the ground and didn't say a word when she felt my presence. I felt the vibe of the room and I knew to sit close to her, so I did. At first, she said nothing and didn't move. I moved closer. I was okay with the silence, and then, this tiny woman, young enough to still have a head full of red hair, takes all her might and she grabs me by my collar and gives me the slap of my lifetime. I mean she slapped me so good I got sober! My entire high was blown.

I jumped off the bed and took some distance from her. She looked me in my eyes and she said, "I am not going to live to see you change or see you become the man that you are striving to become before you got yourself hooked into this. You're going to do the real soul searching and find a good woman for yourself." She continued to say, "You will be a family man. A man that will love God, and you will find yourself, Garry. You can't stay here on earth like this. You will change and make me proud. I know it."

I looked my mom in her glossy eyes and I said, "Mom, you are going to be alright. I will be here when this surgery is over. We both ain't going nowhere." She didn't say another word, she just looked at me. Her look was a look I imagine many people give when they know their time is running out. She didn't give a fake smile, she didn't try to cheer me up, but she gave me that motherly look I knew too well when she was serious.

I never forgot her face, and I will never forget that day. The day was July 25th, 1997. The surgery was to unclog arteries, and it was a success. The only issue, she needed plasma. Based on her convictions she wouldn't receive blood from someone else. There were no alternatives available at this time, and she made no changes to her decision. A few days later, I would say 5 days later, she had a massive heart attack.

The doctors–God worked a miracle and she was brought back. The same day, she had another heart attack that took her breath, and she was revived a second time! She then had a massive stroke, and it was the stroke that would claim her life. My mother was on life support up until the family decided to pull the plug after having the stroke.

I was broken up about this. I couldn't cope with everything she was going through and I tried to blank out all of my emotions. I remember my brothers were also struggling with the reality we all had to face, Big Mama wouldn't be here too much longer. I knew that day in the hospital she was serious, and I never spoke a word about it. I don't think I spoke a word because I wanted it not to be true. I wanted it to have been a bad dream that I would wake up from.

If I couldn't escape this bad, terrible dream, then I didn't want to feel nothing. But just like that slap sobered me, no matter how much I drank or what I did, I could not get high enough to mask my aching heart. I wanted to quit but I couldn't. If I could have changed my life for anyone it would have been my mother. I wanted so badly to make her proud, but I wasn't able to do what she knew would take more time.

It is a strange feeling to know the hour that a person will leave the earth. I had 24 hours to know the hour was coming, I knew the minute even. It was 12pm noon when the plug was pulled and my mom was released from this world into the next. I didn't believe I was ready. I know some of us feel like we aren't ready for the things that happened in our lives, but I am here to tell you, that trusting God through the process is vital-essential for you living in this life.

But what does Daddy say to His children, my brothers and sisters? Many of the things some say, I have said. I have lost my mom, friends, money, status, my life, houses, apartments, clothes, things I had, and nearly my mind. I didn't care for myself, the friends I had, the women I dated, or the hearts I broke because of their disappointment in me. I was a mess family at one point, and I give Daddy all the praise because He has been faithful in taking me through. I want to show you–not just tell you, what it looks like to go through the process.

This isn't about pulling out skeletons in my closet, some things are between me and God, but we overcome by the hearing of each other's testimonies

(Revelation 12:11). Allow me to share some things with you and rest assured, you will see the value of your process. I am also believing you will see why you must go through the storm holding Daddy's hand!

Scripture is the Foundation of Our Faith

We must remember that scripture is the foundation of our faith. It is how we move, breathe, and have our being. The promises of God are yes and amen and they shall come to pass! He said, "Fear not, nor be dismayed: For The LORD God, even my God, will be with thee, He will not fail thee, nor forsake thee" (1 Chronicles 28:20(b).

Also, 2 Corinthians 4:8-9 is truly encouraging, listen: "We are troubled on every side, distressed: we are perplexed, but not in despair. Persecuted, but not forsaken: cast down but not destroyed." GOD GOT US! He got you! He does love us! He does have our absolute best interest in His mind & heart concerning us!

Family, I am excited, but know this isn't the same "song & dance" that has been playing continuously on repeat, but a Rhema Word filled with His real love. This isn't what you may have heard about pre-Covid for some, but it is what many need post-Covid. Many of us have been churched for decades but we had no roots!

Many of us lost loved ones, moms, dads, sisters,

and brothers. This storm snatched us from our shallow holes we were placed in. Emptied us of religion, and showed us what we truly believed by pulling back the curtain on our lives. Whatever we were doing before Covid many waxed worst during and post-Covid. The emptiness of religion is no longer sufficient to keep humanity, so we must get to know Daddy to be able to stand.

We were dead in religion, sleep! We couldn't hear or see a need to believe again like we used to with Big Mama and 'nem'. This generation of so-called adult or mature Christians has no foundation of 'holy love'. What's so scary is many people who believe in holiness are dying off! So much went through the fire during Covid and got burnt up, but God! He can give you beauty for ashes (Isaiah 61:3).

This is that word that the elders (Big Momma & nem) put in your ear. They were feeding you the Word when you were on your way to church with them. Also, when they made you go get the 'switch' (belt), to instill 'the fear of God' in you they did it out of love. We didn't like or understand the process at the time, but many would say that spanking saved their life!

Not all spankings we got were physical either. Have you ever gotten what you needed from a conversation? Yes, my momma slapped the fool out of me from her hospital bed. It shocked me and I thank god it didn't spark an instant reflex because I probably would have died that day too! You know you can't be slapping your momma and get away with that. Old school mommas sick or well will do their best to beat you down.

But again, we would say that the slaps, belts, and switches we saw in our lifetime helped us to get right. Before going to that hospital to see my mom, I was living fast and thought I would die early. Most black men growing up in impoverished, drug-infested, hustling environments learn the rules for surviving the streets. You either master the streets or leave them. To leave took much more faith than playing the role.

I took what at first appeared to be the easy road. I started hanging out, running the streets, and doing what I saw others doing to make money. I loved clothes and looking clean so I knew that cost. I was soo cool, original, I never bought my close in New York where I lived. I didn't want to look like anybody else. I wanted to look and feel like Garry. I remember I would take a bus and go to Canada to shop.

Yes, I was willing to travel to shop but it never occurred to me to travel to make a different life. I guess when you see the fruits of your labor, it can deceive you into believing you are good because of what you have. Although I made bad decisions in my life, I never gave up my heart.

Just as important as looking good, smelling good, and keeping myself was to me, it was equally important that I had a good heart. I remember many times helping single mothers pay their electric bills and rent. Many of these women were on drugs or chasing bad habits, but I never wanted children to suffer. I was so glad my mother spared me from that kind of life and it was something I wouldn't wish on no child's life.

Moments like this gave me the strength I needed to see a glimpse of myself for when I truly lost myself. Have you ever taken a road that you thought you could turn around from, only to realize that road was full of twisted vines? People who started smoking thinking they could stop. Those that tried drinking or drugs, and couldn't stop when they thought they were good and ready. The kind of vines that wrap around your ankles and make each step you take more draining than the next wasn't a part of the picture.

I was always strong in mind and spirit. I never did nothing I didn't want to do and refused to be dominated by anyone. However, I didn't consider a thing that could have me so entangled. Maybe you were like me and you thought you were strong enough by yourself to fight, to stand, to be strong on your own. I fought this battle for many of years to be clean and sober, but it was that day in the hospital that I really started to feel the weight of my decisions.

No, I didn't get it all right at that moment. I had gotten into trouble before and after that. My life wasn't easy, but I am grateful that the Father can make it all work to my good. I believe that what He did in my life, Daddy can do the same in your life. He can pull us up and out of our issues and set us on a path that isn't destruction.

My worst enemy at one time wasn't even the devil, it was myself! Growing up I wanted to outdo myself. As the Bible says, "Hell and destruction are never full; so the eyes of man are never satisfied (Proverbs 27:20)." I was always looking to one-up myself. If I made money, I wanted more. If I was drunk or high, I wanted to be higher. I was never satisfied.

When we are living out of our flesh, we find all too well, we are never satisfied. We will convince ourselves, that our best is not good enough and we think the solution is to dig deep. But that is not it. I was searching for something I don't think many find, but I am grateful I did. I was looking for fulfillment.

I didn't have that in my girl at the time. I didn't have it in my life. I didn't even enjoy being high, I hated it. I wanted to be sober, but not being high was so physically painful and draining. I became a slave to what I thought would set me free! We tell ourselves, oh let me take a drink so I can let loose.

We never think taking a drink, doing a hit, eating another bite, having another partner, or whatever is our vice would lead to an addiction. Would lead us to a lifestyle and a condition we could not control. I was out of control and I didn't know how to reel it back in.

I was around people that also were out of control so watching them didn't help check me, it only affirmed my life decisions. It is a sad day when two addicts compare their lives one to the other. When addicts can sit and be their own judge. But this is what the devil does. He divides to conquer. He has us sit with our thoughts or no thoughts. We can read, "A idle mind is the devil's workshop (Proverbs 16:27)!" But how do we get there?

An idle mind isn't just empty, it is full of thoughts that mean you no good. It is false realizations, deception that we have taken as truth or reality. Time doesn't seem to matter when we are trapped here. Emotions seem to be muted, and our hearts can appear cold.

This is why I'm trusting the process because, from experience, God has shown me how much He truly loves me. Family, when I was growing up, I came from a great family, or at least that was my opinion. I had loving parents, aunts, uncles, siblings, and cousins. To be fair, we could get a bit wild at times but we mean good. Our neighborhood was the typical New York City 1960s or 1970s hood. Everyone knew everyone, folks 'got down, how they got down'!!!

Living a street life never raised sirens in my head to change my life. I remember running down the street one time. I could feel the energy, the heat in my chest as I ran. Sometimes you don't ask questions, but your instincts tell you to run so you do it.

As I was running and I saw others running next to and in front of me, I heard the bullets. I didn't know where to run toward, or in what direction the bullets were coming from, I just felt the unction to run. As I ran and saw the bullets spray seemingly into every inanimate object around me, cars, trees, walls, doors, and windows, I knew I was lucky–but I didn't realize I was blessed!

I should have died that night. I really should have had a closed casket, but not only did I live, but I also wasn't shot! Sometimes we don't know why we are running, from what, or who may be even talking to us, but if you hear run it's best to run. I didn't know God's voice at this time nor did I desire to be a holy roller at the time.

I had no concept of God and I don't remember praying when I went or left the hospital. I left that stuff to the people who had faith. I was a carnal man at the time and I was heavily invested in my flesh. I didn't know to be separated from the Spirit of God, and the presence of God meant I was a participant in the kingdom of darkness.

I was so lost. I didn't realize that my life was not my own, but there was a war happening for my soul (my mind, will, and emotions). All this time, I thought it was all about me and what I wanted. That it was all about what I wanted to do. I felt like I was the man, no matter the condition, this was me and the life I chose.

I didn't see the shift that took place that separated me from being my own to being owned. I was a slave to addiction–and a slave to sin! I was so messed up at the time. I told myself I wanted and enjoyed it. I know this might be too much for y'all super holy saints. I know y'all never made choices you regretted. I am sure you never committed a sin that showed you your humanity and how wicked it is. Maybe you were born with a halo over your head, but I was not.

I was never a man-pleaser. I never saw myself chasing after anything, but I had met my match. It didn't talk, couldn't walk, didn't love me, nor take care of me. But it stole, took, ruined, and discarded me. How many people know what it is like to be deceived, hurt, and feel abandoned–but God!

He can take your ashes and give you beauty (Isaiah 61:3). He can take the balled-up pieces of paper and iron them out, making the crooked paths straight (Isaiah 45:2). My mind, my heart and my soul were crooked. I didn't have a Godly mindset and I had no hunger for it either–But God!

I remember one day, I was high, but I heard a voice. I heard a voice clear as I am talking to you, and it told me, "How long?" I got scared because you know black folks don't do no ghosts. We will hurt ourselves if we think we heard or saw a ghost.

Hearing voices will sober even the highest person up. I got quick fast and a hurry silent and I told the woman I was sitting with what I heard. She laughed and told me I was tripping, but I knew that wasn't the case. I knew I needed to investigate this voice but I wasn't ready.

I kid you not, 2 years to the day, I was sitting at the same table and doing the same things. I heard the same voice ask me again, it was loud enough to where I could hear it over my internal and external noise. It asked me, "How long?"

This time I was scared. I ain't go lie, I was so scared I told the same girl what I heard. Something happened this time. She looked as if she might have heard what I heard. I cannot say if she did or didn't, but something shook in me and I knew it was God. But I had to ask myself was I ready? I wasn't ready family, I ain't go lie at that time. You know how sometimes we need a strong rebuke to get in alignment with God's will?

I got that strong rebuke. I ended up spending some time in prison because I didn't stop running the streets. I was locked up for about 2 years, and it was during that time I stayed sober. I was sober for 2 years and 1 month before I returned home. I was like Moses, I had left home because I was running from trouble, and on my way running from trouble, I ran into the will of God! He fixed me up on the inside, although I didn't know it was Him, I only knew I was grateful. Who would think prison or jail would have a positive impact on your life?

After He fixed me up, He sent me back home. When I went home I didn't know what I was returning for. I didn't know what I was going to, and honestly, I didn't think the people I knew before I wanted to get back close to. So when I got off the bus and took in the air. I just remember thinking, what am I doing here? I started walking up the street heading to the only home I knew, and I saw a car seem to drive past me, slow up, then kept going.

I didn't pay it too much mind, but as I looked up ahead, I saw the car pulled over on the side of the road. I could swear there were at least two passengers in the car, although I wasn't for sure who. I was caught up in my thoughts and the voice I heard seemed familiar but I paid it no mind. As I kept walking I heard my name, she called out to me, "Garry, Garry! Get in." I looked into the car and it was the woman I last knew before leaving town.

I said, "Yo, where boy go. Didn't you have somebody in the car?" She replied, "Yeah, when I saw you, I called out to you, I wasn't sure if you heard me or saw me. I put that dude out and told him to walk home. Man, it has been a minute. How have you been?" We talked for a bit, and I told her about some changes happening in my life, and she said we should go to church one of these days. She had gotten clean too while I was away. Not giving it too much thought, I agreed.

Now I have never thought about going to church. My father's side of the family is thick when it comes to the church. I knew they were big into the church when growing up, but I didn't feed much into it. My mom had her faith, but she didn't push it on us. Much of my family on my mom's side are Jehovah Witnesses and people who did their own thing. This side of the family was surely more wild. I never had a real strong conviction in God growing up so I wasn't sure what to expect going to church.

But that morning I woke up, and she came by the house. We just went to the closest one to where we live. It was no advertisements or anything that we thought pulled us to the church. She just drove and pulled over, then to church we went.

So we arrive at the church and they were in the throws of worship. I came through the double doors, and as soon as I breathed in the air from the room, my knees got weak and I hit the floor. This wasn't a normal drop. I didn't trip, there was nothing on the floor. But something I could not see took over my body. It not only took over my legs, but it also grabbed ahold of my mouth.

I opened my mouth, not of my own accord, but something fell on me. Something–or someone took over and I started speaking in a language I couldn't understand. I did not know what I was doing or saying. I was scared because these words were coming out and I did not know what they meant. People were staring at me and I was staring back at them with worry in my eyes but my mouth kept speaking.

I was still on the floor, I couldn't move. I was compelled to stay there. I was crying my emotions were bursting over and my joy was indescribable. I had missed this feeling and some feelings I was experiencing I had never known before. I didn't know what took a hold of me, but I didn't want it to let me go. It settled my emotions, it cleared my mind, it eliminated my pain, I felt free in the moment–for every minute I was there I was free! I was so light I felt like I could fly.

I didn't know the purpose of going to church or this woman's role in my life at the time. But if I could thank her for anything, it would be for bringing me to church. Perhaps that was the purpose of our meeting, to bring me to this moment?

He Has a Purpose for Your Life

This is a fact family… God has a purpose for each and every one of us living in this dying world. He has a specific process, however, that He uses for His Glory & our benefit that must be followed. Listen family, at this juncture, the entire human race, which is actually created in God's image & likeness has the choice to turn away from God. We were created to love & worship Him but through the fall of Adam, the plans changed because man didn't follow their divine assignment.

God desires for us to love, honor, praise, glorify, & bless His holy name. According to the scriptures, the enemy of God & man is satan (and fallen angels) and he has "blinded the minds of them which believeth not (2 Corinthians 4:4)." He has destroyed the earth with sin by putting the 'human race' against God, against one another, and against the earth itself!

Yeah, our problems–all of our problems stem from the principalities of darkness influence on man. Whether they are demons, evil spirits, or the devil, these entities attempt to interfere with our life circumstances. Their goal is to deceive man and get us to give in to our base nature which was shaped in iniquity (sin) after the fall. Here's a word of encouragement that I had with DADDY that I want to share with you. Again, I call Him that because that's who He is to me. He is my divine Father. He's closer to me than anyone or anything. To call Him God at times is too distant and not personal enough for me. There are many gods, but only one Divine. Only one Creator of all things and He calls me son, the least I can do is call Him Daddy!

Have you ever wanted to be quiet in His presence? You know quiet because, in any conversation, two people have to be talking. It can't be one person saying everything, and even if one person talks more, the other has to listen for there to be a real conversation! Do you listen for God's response? Do you allow Him to speak to you? Maybe it is just me, sometimes I get into His presence, and I know I enter with thanksgiving and praise first. I want to reduce how much I speak so that I can hear Him, but I am compelled to honor Him. To give Him what He deserves. Getting into His presence–for me, works like this:

Original journal entry, entitled "Daddy"
DADDY, I just wanna sit here a moment. I just wanna be totally engulfed in Your presence. Dad, I did say, I wanna just sit here but I, I can't help myself. I wanna be quiet, I wanna be still, but I just can't help myself! I wanna Bless You and I wanna keep thanking You. I want You to kno' LORD, that I LOVE YOU!!!

I'm grateful that You remembered me when not only did I, but everyone else forgot about me. When I wasn't a thought in anyone's mind, not even a spot in their hearts, an image on a picture in their homes or on their phones.

DADDY, I just wanna sit here a moment. I just wanna be totally engulfed in Your presence. I wanna thank You for not allowing me to be wiped off the face of the earth before I can let You kno', my Lord, about how much I truly love, honor, adore, and appreciate YOU! Oh, GREAT KING!!! (though I truly deserve death), with ALL of my jack'd-up ways, faults, insecurities, schemes (of mind), but YOU, YOU OH LORD YOU through THE BLOOD, never held my sins against me.

While I sit here, tears running down my beard, my heart is sooooooo full of gratitude. I have a gang of feelings & a 'tribe' of thoughts, that I'm absolutely not able to put into words, let alone on paper. My words can't describe how Your Grace & Your Mercies are far more than I deserve–yet, You still love me!

I can't stop crying. DADDY, I just wanna sit here, for just a moment to thank You for Your love. I'm speechless, though my hand is moving automatically to jot down this "moment in my prayer closet." DADDY, I have to, I must THANK YOU, THANK YOU FOR EVERYTHING!!!!

Oh, LORD! You've given Your Word to allow us to get to know "Your mind" and who YOU are. You've allowed us to have the most precious gift of all... JESUS CHRIST! To bring man, to bring me (Garry), back to you!!! I'm indebted always to YOU GREAT KING JEHOVAH, for thinking of me before You allowed my momma to meet my daddy…

I'm stopping right here…My joy doesn't stop and neither does my tears from flowing. I'm not apologizing for it, I'm just saying just in case my words don't read right or the reader of this sees some dried-up tear stains or some smudged-up words…DADDY, I'm just thanking YOU, as I just sit here for a moment. I am wanting to be totally engulfed in Your presence.

These words are just in my heart. Here I go once again, talking aloud because there's soooooo much that's bubbling forth and I can't help myself! Each time, every time, I think of You Master, I just burst out in WORSHIP, PRAISE, REJOICING, LAUGHTER OF SPIRIT & HEART, CRYING tears of pure joy. Yeah, crying seems to be a great part of our conversations. But WORSHIP… "You ALWAYS lead the way" & I always end with CELEBRATING YOU, GREAT GOD!!!

I just wanna sit here a moment… I just wanna be totally engulfed in Your presence…

Garry Washington

When I was young I used to write poetry, but I let it die in me. I kept my lines in my head, but now, when I spend time with Daddy, I get to express my love for writing. To be writing this book–and how I talk sprinkled in here and there, is a blessing family. I never thought I would be here.

I remember, when I lost it all, not once, not twice, but a few times, and He always kept me through the process. I had to realize my process didn't start when I came to Him, it started before I was born or thought of. Before we came here, our Father in heaven knew us, appointed us, and called us to a purpose (Jeremiah 1:5). This purpose He has predestined since the beginning of time is why we are here. If we trust His process, we will see the manifestation of that purpose!

No, it doesn't matter where you are now, He will work all things to your good! But you don't believe me, do you? You want to bury your past, skip it, and pretend it never happened. If you do this you are missing a key to your process! You have to acknowledge your faults, so you can see and understand what He has done in and for you!

When He called the Hebrews out of Egypt, delivered them from the Pharoah, and gave them a new land flowing with milk and honey. Why do you think He kept reminding them of back-when many times in the Bible? Even in the New Testament–today in our lives, we hear about this account, but why? Because we miss how much we owe Him if we skip over what He brought us from!

But maybe I am the only one that has been brought through? Maybe I am the only one that God had to reach in and pull out! Maybe I am the only one that thought I would be dead by 16. But I lived! Then I thought surely by 21, then I lived. I made it to 30, then I thought okay, death is around the corner–but I lived!

I hit 35 and I said, 'Wait a minute, there must be something to this. I am still here!' I was not in my best shape. I had problems. I had demons I couldn't shake. Problems I was scared to face!

I had debts I couldn't pay and an addiction I couldn't shake. I was messed up. I thought I was doing good strangely, even though I had no fruit. Do you think you are good enough too? I had a woman who thought I was good enough at the time.

I would think surely if I am not alone, that means I am doing something right. I was so wrong family. My wife today and the woman I was dating is leaps and bounds different. The truth, the me back then didn't deserve the wife I have today. Can you be as honest with yourself to say, "Daddy I don't deserve your goodness" and actually mean it?

I cry because my tears are a testament of thanks for my wife. She is the best gift I have gotten after becoming a joint-heir with Christ! To have someone to live with me, love on me, and see me for who I am is something family I can't put in the best words–but I will try. I am not comparing her with any woman, but I do recognize and appreciate what she did and does for me that no other woman has done. When I tell you about why I spoil my wife you will understand. Same as how Christ loves the church, I do love my wife.

Let me tell you what you want to know, ya'll know how I can get sometimes. To the matter at hand. So I had this girl that was still on a track that didn't change after sitting and listening to the service. I was in it following what seemed like every word from the pastor. I was mesmerized because of my experience but

I wanted to be sure this was the real thing and not no hoax.

Before I left the church I was given a Bible to study. I remember studying every day it seemed. I was wanting to learn, I was curious more than anything. I kept going to that church too. But after leaving church for her things between us were not the same. She started mocking my journey calling me "God-man" but in a condescending way. She drew further away from me as I grew closer to Jesus, Daddy.

Have you ever wanted to take people with you on your journey and realized they couldn't go? I mean it is not like they weren't invited, they just didn't have the heart, desire, to want to go. Many times I have met people in my life who like what God has to offer but they don't want to serve Him. They are enjoying their life as-is and to follow Him would take them from that.

I know what it is like, I am sure you may vaguely remember what it was like for you before you were saved. It can be a lonely journey when we have to walk alone and the person we thought would be there is gone. I grew closer to the church and I watched. I wanted to see if these cats were for real. I mean anybody can read the Bible, tell stories, engage an audience, but it takes special power to live what you preach.

I studied and watched for months, and that pastor, who I found out later was my cousin, really practices what he preaches. I remember going to a BBQ one day in support of the church. My mouth was hurting real bad, so I didn't want to be there because I was in pain. But if I give my word I am going to show up, I am going to do my best to be there.

So I am there, sitting and doing my best to chill out. The sun is beaming down the weather was fantastic but the last thing on my mind is smelling food. I tried to stay as far away from where it looked like they would set up the grill as possible. I was staring off into the distance like they do in movies, and a woman came up to me. She tapped me on my shoulder and I turned around. She said, "Excuse me, you think you can help me out a second?"

At first thought, I was going to say, "Naw, I can't help you." But something inside of me knew better, so I replied, "Yeah, I can help. What you need me to do?" She encouraged me to walk with her and I didn't know for a second where we were going. We ended up in front of the last place I wanted to be.

She asked me to help her set up the grill for her and I wondered if she was going to ask me to help cook too! I hadn't eaten red meat since 2001, to this day I still don't eat it. It's been like 20 years. Now y'all know I was saved, but I was in my feelings, I was in pain! I still tried to help her out but I was frustrated, and probably taking it out on the grill and such. I remember she nudged me away from the grill and she started putting the pieces together herself.

I remember thinking, 'Now if she could do this herself, why did she bother me in the first place? My mouth is hurting, I am just trying to sit down and relax." She wasn't finished though. I walked away from the setup grill that she put together and sat back down. She came over to me several minutes later and asked, "Do you want something to eat?"

I responded, a little frustrated to be honest, "Naw, my mouth hurting. I am good." She walked back over to the grill and kept cooking. After a while, she walked back up to me with a chicken wing in hand. I don't like chicken wings, never been my thang. She set the plate down near me and encouraged me to try it. I let it sit there for a minute, but the smell did catch my attention.

I was curious, nosey to be honest, I have always been a bit nosey. So I tasted the tip of that wing and I tell you, 'It was the best chicken wing I have had in my life!' I was damaged but I couldn't stop eating. I couldn't be rude to her, I felt a little bad for how I treated her, so I planned to apologize. Before I could get up to find her, she came back to me and said, "So how was it?"

"It was good thanks very much, Sis!" She didn't leave though. She sat at the table and wanted to talk and keep engaging but mind you, I am still in pain. So I said to get out of it, "Why don't I just call you when my mouth isn't hurting so much? Give me your number and I will call you." I was thinking to call her, chop it up, and then it would be done. I was so busy chasing God and trying to become what I believe my momma always saw in me, that I had no time for women.

I kid you not, I gave this woman a call and I have been talking to her every day for the past 15 years! When my pain went away, and I could be my authentic self, I loved every moment of her time. I love you, Shirl.

Coming to Know Him

Through it all, right now, the only process that I can identify with is The Process Of God, which has brought me through, as I'm going through now. From a little boy until I was in my 40's, I didn't know of God's process or any process for "life." The process of trusting God is something we (I) learned before I could trust God's process. I had to come to know Him so I can determine if He was worthy to be trusted (thank you JESUS). I had to work with very little faith–if any while I was learning of Him, but these were baby steps I had to make so I could develop a relationship with Him.

I wasn't in love with Jesus when I first came to Daddy. In fact, I was skeptical. I came from two sides of the fence. I had a mom who believed in God. She tried her best to make me mind growing up. It wasn't that I didn't hear her, I just didn't–being transparent, value her opinion as much as I did my own. My mom told me much of what the Big Mama's used to tell their sons. You know, "Find yourself a good woman," "Stay away from them nonsense friends you got. They mean you no good." My mom was good, but there was a part of me that didn't want to listen. I did everything I was big and bad enough to do as I told you.

On my mother's side again was a strong presence of Jehovah's Witnesses and believing in your own values. I would say most of my family had a cherry-picked faith system. This understanding and approach to God had charged my siblings, and all my cousins to believe in a way that I was crazy to believe like I do.

Having parents of two different faiths, with each having strong convictions in their beliefs, was always hard on me. I wanted to please them both, but they both believed in a higher power, the lifestyle in which the two lived was very different. I remember my cousins thought I was going to drop the act of worshiping God like I do after a few months.

I would come to the cookouts, attend the events the family was throwing, and of course talk about how good Daddy was to me. None of them understood me. They laughed at me, stopped inviting me to the events, and now I am only called when someone wants something. I am estranged from most of my siblings because my lifestyle to them is too much.

This is something that not only my family members do, but also some of my Christian brothers and sisters. It is amazing how some people want your anointing, your blessings, but they don't want the process of Trusting God to get it themselves. Often I felt and feel alone…

Original journal entry, entitled "When I Feel Alone"

Most Times, I Feel Alone;
I have a wonderful wife, loving family & friends… a good job, also my health is well; But most times, I feel alone…

I'm in love with Jesus & I do have a loving & personal relationship with Him… But most times, I feel alone…

I consider myself (I'm not conceited) an outgoing person… Good sense of humor, jovial, as The LORD is my witness, I try to do right by everyone, without deceit or prejudice to anyone…

I do my best to make a sincere effort to go out of my way to assist whoever I can…

But most times, I feel alone…

What is this that I'm saying? Do I think I'm "all dat" but I'm actually nothing at all… Is my mind psych'n me out? I believe I'm "walk'n the line of Jesus." Let me tell you; perhaps you'll be able to understand just a bit of why Most Times, I Feel Alone. I love The LORD, 4real. So when my "imperfections" show up (which is daily), my heart goes into "panic mode", my mind goes to wondering, "Am I, Can I, Will I, Do the right thing"?

When I see a total disregard by "folks" who "proclaim with a loud voice" that they're in love with my LORD & their very calculated thoughts & actions are different than what they said… Different than mine towards The LORD…Could the same be said about me?

When what is absolutely "wrong" is their normal and they have no remorse. Let that not be true, or possibly said about me Jesus!

(OH, I MEANT TO TELL YOU, THIS IS FOR JESUS LOVERS & THOSE CHASING HIM, 4REAL)...

When what is total scriptural, is taken as "WELLLLL" or that's not applicable for today's standards, because you see, those were the "old standards for the Israelites & first-century church. When the "truth" is a lie & the "lie" is the truth… God help us! If my mate is getting on my nerves, I can "dis" them & get someone else is the rationale. Oh, well it didn't work out is what they say, they file a separation or get a divorce decree later on…

WHAT DID YOU PROCLAIM, YOU SAID, YOU'RE A "SAINT-OF-GOD."

You have no problem being an adulterer, backbiter, fornicator, aggravator, thieving, lying, whoring with any & everybody, homosexual, lesbian, pedophile practicing all kinds of lawlessness–but you say you believe. True believers, I tell you stand alone… (I'm not just being opinionated, this is FACTUAL in The House of Prayer). Yes, these mindsets are not only prevalent in the world, but they have crept into the church!

I CAN'T, I JUST CAN'T…

This is why "Most Times, I Feel Alone"…

When my intentions are right and my motives

are correct. When my actions don't line up with what the purpose of my heart is or when my steps slip, my thoughts get sway'd, I instantly have to pray…

When your absolute isn't absolute; when your swinging & you get knock'd down, emotionally, financially, mentally, in your health, or spiritually… When your look'n about, when your search'n, or call'n out, DADDY (JESUS), but cha' get no response… Those are the moments I say, "Most Times, I Feel Alone" …

The second half of one of my favorite scriptures is this; "I will be with thee: I will not fail thee, nor forsake thee" (Joshua 1:5'b') (I got happy, I had to do a quick shout to show my "gratitude.) I'm back now…

When The LORD brings back to my heart His promises towards me, I get revived… I know I am not alone because He is with me. If He is silent, whispering, talking, or allowing His glory to hover. I know He is here with me. I know if I don't see people, or if I stand on the other side of popularity, That I–no "WE WILL MAKE IT!!" For those that at times feel like me, you are not alone…

This Is My Expression Of One Of Those Times

"When I Feel Alone"

Garry Washington

It was not easy coming to know God. It feels like once you get past that honeycomb stage at the beginning of the relationship, the real work kicks in. You know where you have to fight to take a step, to gain a mile, when it used to come easier. I had a house, a place, food on the table, and all the necessities before I got real deep in God.

I remember having a car and being able to get around and run around town. I was able to keep a job to support my moves, and I loved this new space I was in. I was happy with Shirl and things seemed to be looking up in my life. I got stuff I didn't ask for or wasn't expecting.

Many of y'all know the honeycomb phase and when it seems like your world shifts. Like elevation comes with a test in God. This is why I always believed, be careful what you ask for or desiring to have what someone else got. You don't know what it cost them to get there.

I remember Shirl and I dated for about 8 months before we got married. I was so happy with her. She made life easier on me, but when we got married, it was like the gates of hell came up against us! We had financial problems, we had car problems, we had food problems, we had spiritual challenges, and we got the looks that called us crazy.

I remember we would go to church and people would treat us like they didn't want to get too close to us in case whatever we had could jump off of us and hit them. I am not talking about the pastor, or the few that cared, but many that filled the seats separated themselves from us. They didn't want nothing to do with us and I am sure blamed us for what we were going through.

Have you ever been going through a test with God and people saw the test as your fault? Of course, we can point to Job in the Bible and understand how man thinks. He was a faithful servant, doing everything right for the most part–to the point where the devil and God had no fault in him.

The devil said, "The only reason Job is faithful is because you put a hedge of protection around him. Who wouldn't serve you if you protected them and never let a real test knock at their door." You know I am paraphrasing the situation, I pray you don't mind. So God gave the devil permission to try His servant Job. The devil hit Job in his body, with his children, his wife turned against him, and his friends accused him.

Job was so down he started to curse his very existence! He cursed the day he was born, the breast of his mother for feeding him, and he separated himself from his friends, his wife, and his children died! He had boils on his skin, it was painful and nasty. It made my toothache seem like lying on the beach with a tropical fruity drink in my hand with an umbrella, and no alcohol.

Our brotha was going through! On top of this, his friends kept saying, "You need to repent. You brought this misfortune on yourself. Why are you suffering if you didn't do anything wrong?" Reminds you also of an account in the New Testament when Jesus said something like this in John 9:3, "It was not because of his sins or his parents' sins," Jesus answered. "This happened so the power of God could be seen in him." You see some of us are struggling, going through for

Daddy's glory!

Not everyone is in a low place because they brought it on themselves. For some of us, it is for the Father's glory or because He bragged about us! He wants us to know Him deeply, intimately, and closer than a brother, father, mother, or even a spouse. How are we supposed to know him so well if we ain't been through nothing?

If you have never been challenged or seen a problem, how would you know how big God is? How would you know Him as powerful, if He never moved a muscle for you? How would you know him as healer, if you don't know about HIm healing? How do you know Him as deliverer, if nobody has been delivered! The Bible is great for giving us testimonies, and accounts of God's character, but there comes a time when we must be a living testament. Where we must continue the work that Jesus started, Kingdom work.

We would never appreciate, nor be able to tell others with conviction how good God is if we have never trusted Him through a process. I mean a real process, not a quick get out of jail card. My wife and I went through and we did it together. That is a gift from God not to have to go through this life alone. Not to have to work out everything by yourself. But for two to come together and become one flesh for the fulfillment of Godly purpose!

I remember when our lights got cut off. We had a terrible neighbor. She never spoke to us. She would give us a stank eye. Wanted to call the police on us about how we parked our cars, just anything to be a nuisance. When our lights got cut off I promise it felt like I could feel her grin across the street.

But we had no intentions of making our situation known to others. We didn't tell people at church much of nothing because we were already blackballed. We didn't want to isolate ourselves even more or keep bringing up problem after problem. I mean let's be real, who wants a friend that every time you talk to them it is a new problem? We didn't want to be a burden to people and we didn't want to be anyone's problem.

But something happened that day that we never thought would have. It was a super hot day. I mean it felt like 400 degrees outside. It was so hot. Being in the house was worse than being outside. Have you ever been so hot you felt like getting mad about the simplest of things? Anything could tick you off, so it was best you just sat outside.

While we were sitting outside, our next-door neighbor who didn't talk much to us came over to us this day. She said, "I don't know why I was led to go to the store and pick up these cords. But I did. I plugged them in at my house and I was told to bring this part to you. So I am bringing them. Whatever you need to do with them, please do. They will remain plugged in until you bring them back to me." She put the plugs in my hand and she walked off!

It is always a heartwarming feeling when Daddy wraps His arms around you. When you can feel His Spirit, even when you may think you can't see Him. He is there with you in the thick of it. He is there with you through the process. He says He will never leave you nor forsake you. He says He will stick with you closer than a brother. He truly has stuck with us, and it is during these low times, that Shirl and I learned so much about the nature, the goodness, and the faithfulness of God.

We had our refrigerator on, we didn't have AC, but those fans felt like ice sicles in that house. We could cook and eat. We didn't lose our food. We were blessed at our lowest moment, by an unexpected host. We were truly touched by her generosity and it was to God's glory that she gave and we were able to receive.

Never think what you have is too little to please God. She didn't pay our bill, but she gave us what we needed. Sometimes it is giving out of your poverty that means the most to God. When the widow gave her two mince, Jesus said, she gave more than everyone giving out of their plenty. Because giving out of her poverty cost her more, because it meant more to her.

We are to be cheerful givers. We are to smile and be merry when we give, tithe, or do anything out of love. It is what you do out of the Spirit of Love, which is who God is, that matters. The Bible says God is Love. So we ought to love and show love when we do the work of the ministry, the work of the Kingdom of God. That woman blessed us, so much she is in my book! I am grateful for her obedience.

I remember one time we were getting evicted from an apartment we lived in. I mean sheriff showed up and they were moving things around to begin their motion of throwing your stuff out. You know when those boys get started, they don't care how your stuff lands outside. They toss it straight out the door without a care. To make it worst, there is nothing you can say usually to get them to stop once they get started.

As Shirl and I stood there, always praying, remaining hopeful, out of the blue, someone from the front office came running toward our unit. She said, "Stop, stop, they are good." The men's heads were down and one of them looked up to see her running down the road. He stuck his head out of the house to check on what she was yelling.

She said it again, "Stop, stop! They are good. Their rent is paid. They good." The two men were a bit confused, and I also think embarrassed, walked out of the house a bit slumped over. The office lady said to us, "Apologies for not getting this message out to you sooner, but your rent is paid." She turned away and walked away. Shirl and I looked at each other, we never knew who paid our rent.

We weren't trying to stop the process, we were watching it unfold, BUT GOD! He stopped them from throwing all of our items on the curb. He allowed us to witness a miracle and benefit again from His grace. To the person or persons who gave to us, thank you!

Sometimes we don't know when Daddy will send us a person or an angel, but if we believe, all things are possible! We had no health insurance for years. You know how scary it can be to have issues with no insurance. My wife and I had no problems when we were uninsured. We didn't have back problems, serious illnesses, or a reason to go to the hospital. We were good by His Grace!

Growing Your Relationship with God

Now, amid our growing relationship, I started falling in love with Him. Today, I trust Him because I have been through too much with Him not too! I started as a babe like all of us do, and I am now an elder, but I had a process to endure to get here. I can tell you if I kept the same friends or relationships I had in my past, I would not be here. To get us to elevate in God sometimes means leaving people behind that cannot follow us.

Do you remember when Jesus went into the room to resurrect a child who had died or He said was sleeping? He had 12 disciples, a crowd of folks that witnessed His miracles, but they all could not come into the room. He kicked them out! Sometimes people have to follow you from a distance and they cannot be close.

Some will fall away altogether and never be with you again. When JESUS went into the room He only invited the ones who had the same heart, same mind, and same spirit to enter that room. He wanted people that believed in the process that was about to unfold.

Matthew 9:23-25 recounts the story:

When Jesus entered the house of the synagogue leader, He saw the flute players and the noisy crowd. 24 "Go away," He told them. " The girl is not dead, but asleep." And they laughed at Him. 25 After the crowd had been put outside, Jesus went in and took the girl by the hand, and she got up.

He kicked out those that would be a stumbling block. The naysayer, those that live and operate in doubt. Sometimes to find these people you don't have to look far. You just have to look at your inner circle or the crowd around you. Don't be afraid to kick people out that are not part of your process. We will never fulfill the purpose nor see the miracles, if we are not in the right room or company.

I could tell you some wild stories about what I have seen the power of JESUS do in the natural. I can't tell you how many times I have seen demons running around people's houses. The smell of a demon I can notice from the smell of stink.

When you walk with God, He can give you assignments that many others are not ready to take on. I am not talking about a Seven sons of Sceava response either. You know when people have a form of godliness and power? That is how it is when people play with God's gifts thinking they are toys. Too many people have gotten hurt trying to be something they are not. Claiming to believe when they do not.

Acts 19:11-16 has the account:

11 God gave Paul the power to perform unusual miracles. 12 When handkerchiefs or aprons that had merely touched his skin were placed on sick people, they were healed of their diseases, and evil spirits were expelled. 13 A group of Jews was traveling from town to town casting out evil spirits. They tried to use the name of the Lord Jesus in their incantation, saying, "I command you in the name of Jesus, whom Paul preaches, to come out!"

14 Seven sons of Sceva, a leading priest, were doing this. 15 But one time when they tried it, the evil spirit replied, "I know Jesus, and I know Paul, but who are you?" 16 Then the man with the evil spirit leaped on them, overpowered them, and attacked them with such violence that they fled from the house, naked and battered.

When we play around with what we believe–faking until you make it doesn't work with God and it doesn't work on demons, the devil, or evil spirits either. You have to know Him before you try and cast out a demon or that same devil could come upon you! If we don't have the power of the Spirit of God, the Word of God (Jesus), we find ourselves naked and unable to stand in the face of evil powers.

I remember my wife and I were called out to a house by a member of the church. This was one of the same ones, that looked down on us when we were going through, but now, we are the ones that the Almighty raised up to pray for them. Don't be so quick to judge a person by their process, you don't know what God is going to do until He is done. Let Him finish the work on that person and in you, before you throw your hands up and call them a waste.

So we get the call and we head over to the house. As soon as we hit the door, the smell hits me straight in my nose. I look at Shirl, and she looks at me, we both are like a dynamic duo, especially in the spirit. We can communicate with our eyes, a touch, or a smile. We are connected, not perfect, but we love and are committed to each other. There is no such thing as a perfect marriage, but there are plenty of examples of a purpose-filled one. I have that!

So we step into the house, and I don't know about you, but we feel the weight of the room. When a spirit is living somewhere the room feels heavy, the stink rises, and you know you have been instantly put into a spiritual battlefield. Not all demons are ghosts and images you can't see, sometimes they manifest themselves through people or independently.

I saw this demon and it talked to me. I went up to the brother struggling and I began to call on the name of JESUS! The demon wanted to introduce himself and say why he felt he could stay. As my wife prayed, and the presence of God filled the room, the demon said my name is " Ekhial." I remember as clear as crystal. My short-term memory is not so good, but the long term is sharp as a tack! I told that spirit he had to go, he must leave, he had no authority to remain in my presence.

I am a witness that the same power that Paul had, that Jesus had, we have it today! I am also a living witness, that the demons that beat up the seven sons of Sceava, are still here, and they can mess you up if you are not filled. When that demon came out of that man he bumped into me!

I don't mean no tap, he shoved past me as he went out the door! I would have been shocked if this was my first time, but it wasn't. The power of God was on me, working through me, and alive, so the devil could not harm me. I was in another house doing the same thing with Shirl, praying and casting out spirits.

In one house it was these little creatures that were present. I saw them as clearly as I can see a dog. They stood no taller than a foot tall, but they were aggressive. I rebuked them and they left. These creatures are wild-looking, their hair is all over the place, and I think some people call them nymphs. They are some nasty little creatures that bring out all kinds of problems in people's lives. Trust me, family, you don't want to live with demons, evil spirits, and the devil, you want to cast them out!

The devil is not a friend, a brother, or nothing like the Lord. He is not the opposite of God, he is no match! He doesn't own nothing–hell doesn't even belong to him. It is the Lord's. The earth belongs to God and everything that is in it, above, or below it. So why do people sell their souls, and give up their will, mind, and emotions to the kingdom of darkness I do not understand. This kingdom is lower than the earth, it is in hell!

And hell wants to manifest on earth, using you

and I to get here. They will try and use an animal, doll, or anything to be amongst the living. They are dead because God killed them back in Genesis when they tried to mate and live with man. Enoch can tell you all about it, but I'm telling you, God is deep and His power immeasurable.

When you are operating in power you see some things! I remember my wife called me when I was at work. "She said Garry, you won't believe it. I just killed a snake in the kitchen."

Now you and I both know snakes don't live in the north like they do in Florida. Snakes ain't trying to be nowhere near our house. It is cold, snowing, ain't no snakes. But I believe my wife and I know if she killed a snake, she killed a snake.

So I kept working and a few hours later she calls me back and she says, "I killed a dragon!" I was like what a dragon? And she continued to say in a hurried voice, "I killed the dragon and stuff came all over my arms. I have to clean up my hands!"

I was like wow! Daddy, what kind of battling is this? We ain't got no supernatural talk show, we regular people, living like you, but with God supernatural things we can witness. But these things I would have never known, if I didn't get close to God.

I've learned & still am learning about His marvelous heart towards me. To show me things, His love, His power, His grace, His patience. Once I developed a true relationship with Jesus (the way The LORD wants the relationship to be), then that's when trusting Him became 'a way of life'. That is called "FAITH," Did you know, "Without faith, it is impossible to please God" (Heb 11:6).

So, for us to "Trust Gods' Process (As We're Going Through)," we must believe. To believe, we must allow ourselves to have a relationship with God. But first, we have to get to know Him…

So again, to trust the process of God as we're going through anything & everything, we must have faith in God that in every circumstance we know He's there. When you are in a hospital room, lying in your bed and you can't get up. When you see spirits dancing around your room, or if you hear noises.

Trusting God is also believing in "spiritual realities." God is a Spirit and He is so able to fight that battle for you and silence voices, thoughts, ideas, and manifestations. Learn to trust or keep trusting His power!

Obeying His Commands

Trusting God's Process is also obeying His commands. You cannot say you love someone you don't listen to. Likewise, you cannot communicate with anyone if only one person does all the talking and listening. To have an effective conversation both parties must speak and listen at the appropriate times.

When I pray sometimes I can spend the entire time worshiping, giving thanks for what God has done, but I realized I wasn't leaving much room for Him to talk back to me when I started my journey. Can you relate? Have you ever been so excited that your mouth keeps moving and you don't give the other person time to speak? I know of a few conversations where I asked the question, answered, and closed the topic of discussion afterward.

When you ask God a question, do you wait on Him to give you an answer? When I was new in the faith I didn't have that much patience. I guess too, we can be afraid of what He may give us as the solution so we rush to our own thoughts? But the Bible tells us, "Don't lean on our own understanding (Proverbs 3:4)." I was guilty of this in the beginning though.

I know sometimes we can have this Bible and think, I know the Word, so I will do what I see here. Sometimes we mingle the Word with the world and think that the outcome should be alright. Only later to learn it wasn't alright. It was a problem and soon a big problem would unfold because of our decision.

I had to learn to quiet myself to hear from God. When I first heard His voice, I wasn't even saved. I wasn't sure if it was a ghost, my voice in my head, or what. When I started working on a relationship with God, I wanted to learn His voice. I fell in love with the verse, "My sheep know my voice, and no other will they hear (John 10:27)."

I wanted to live like this, be like this, hear like this! So I remember praying for it. I prayed and not that I didn't think God would do it, but how He did it was amazing. I remember when I first started hearing the Voice of God. It wasn't super loud in my ears. It didn't feel like the clouds moved back and a booming voice came on like in the movies. It was a still voice, talking to me like I would talk to you if we were in the same room. I can hear Him like that.

First I would get this feeling. I would feel His presence and I knew the voice to follow was His. When He would speak I would shut up. I would try to keep my thoughts clear, and before I would pray I started to clear my mind of worry, thoughts, or ideas so I couldn't drown out His voice. I would sit and wait on the Lord. Just because we sit down to talk to God doesn't mean He is ready to talk. Sometimes He wants to talk when I wasn't praying!

I can't tell you how many times I was in the truck driving and the Spirit would fall on me, I would feel His presence and then hear His voice. Now that I know His voice, I can hear Him without the feeling. God is not just a feeling, but He is a knowing that cannot be as easily put into words. When you know His voice, no one can talk you out of it.

Another thing, when you hear conversations in your head, meaning a voice asking a question and getting an answer, you need to think about who am I communicating with. Yes God speaks, and so do demons, devils, and yourself. You want to be sure you are hearing God, and you know that you are by the Spirit it brings.

The Bible makes sure we are not confused by His Spirit, because He gave us what the fruits of His Spirit are in Galatians 5:22-23. It reads, "But the fruit of the Spirit is love, joy, peace, longsuffering, gentleness, goodness, faith, meekness, temperance: against such, there is no law." When you operate out of the Fruits of the Spirit, as far as Godliness, you will find that your actions will adhere to the heavenly design.

When we are operating out of our thoughts, entitlements, or beliefs, the fruits of that spirit will not be expressed. Are you puffed up in your mind? Can people tell you anything? Can you be corrected? Will you humble yourself if you are right or wrong to establish understanding?

Some people in life feel they must be dead right. They want to be right more than they value a relationship, or the ability to usher a soul to Christ. As believers operating with the Spirit, sure we know the answer, but for some, you have to hear them out, be patient, so that you can meet people where they are. Can you imagine, if before you were born again, saved, holy-ghost filled, and you came to Jesus and asked Him questions about your life? For many of us, Daddy almost had to put a gag over our mouths to stop us from over-talking His truth to compare it to our experiences.

Everybody loves joy and peace. We all want it. Joy for most of us may be confused with happiness. Happiness is a state of being happy with how things are going in a current circumstance. We all want to be happy. Many people think that happiness is grounds for divorce, given up, given in, or given out.

Family, joy is the power that comes from on High that will hold you up when the circumstances don't feel good. We can celebrate Him because we know it won't last always! With God on the throne, He will call forth the sun to push away the rain.

But if I am only concerned about my happiness, I will never fully embrace Joy! Because Joy comes in the morning. Love, love is trivial and often confused in our modern society. We say we love pizza, video games, this or that, but love is so much more than that. Many of us throw around the word love, like how we use the words "like very much."

To Love is so much deeper than the word Like. You can like something, but you won't suffer for something you like. You will let it go when something gets too tough. You will say I will just pick another one if that item is out of stock. But love will make you go without.

It will make you leave a store, a house, country and stay focused to find it elsewhere. Abraham heard the voice of God and he loved God. He loved Daddy so much, that he obeyed Him and left his entire family behind in search of his promise. Love will make you completely unsatisfied with the others, to a point where you will not want another.

When we truly understand love, love makes us picky. Selective and it causes us to value a thing more than anything else. The Bible says that God is Love (1 John 4:8), but what else:

"7 Beloved, let us love one another, for love is from God, and whoever loves has been born of God and knows God. 8 Anyone who does not love does not know God, because God is love. 9 In this the love of God was made manifest among us, that God sent his only Son into the world, so that we might live through him.

10 In this is love, not that we have loved God but that he loved us and sent his Son to be the propitiation for our sins. 11 Beloved, if God so loved us, we also ought to love one another. 12 No one has ever seen God; if we love one another, God abides in us and his love is perfected in us. 13 By this we know that we abide in him and he in us, because he has given us of his Spirit."

To love is to know and see God. We should not

be so cavalier to say whom we love if we in fact don't. The concept of "puppy love" is so false. Love is something more than a heartstring, emotion…or craving! It is a conscious decision, commitment, intelligent and calculated decision.

God the Father, Creator, did not send His Son to earth because he had a sensation. He sent Him because He was intentional. He was committed to His purpose. He wanted man to be reconnected with His Spirit and took His Son to bring Him here again to dwell within in man.

Love will have you give of yourself! It will cause you to dig deep, reflect, sacrifice, and be long-suffering. Long-suffering is bearing whatever may come to accomplish a sacrificial act. Beatings, crucifixion, hell, and ascension came for JESUS to redeem us and HE did it!

He not only came here to heal us, feed us, but also to deliver, redeem, and restore us! He was the example we could not be for ourselves. He proves the Word true, and He is the Word made flesh (John 1:14).

The kindness is indescribable. It is impossible to bear the fruit of Daddy's Spirit and not be kind. We have to demonstrate love because love is the most powerful weapon. Love cast out hate, and it brings light that cast out the darkness.

Have you ever tried to rehabilitate a rejected dog? You know, like a dog that was abused by its previous owners? Usually, they can start either timid, aggressive, or unpredictable. But the more love, patience, goodness, kindness, you show this dog, you can change this dog's heart.

Now all animals are not the same, and neither are all people. Sometimes, people don't want to be loved. Hence, not everyone wants God! How sad is that life? A life void of love? You can be in relationships, run companies, have animals, and all kinds of stuff.

But to live life without love you only feel used. Because you will eventually feel that people want you for your stuff because love is not in it. This is why many people don't mind leaving you when those things are gone.

Are you gentle? Have you ever seen a dog, that won't share his food? They are so aggressive, they will bite their owner, who feds them if they try and get close to their food! Are you like that?

You grit your teeth, growl, and stand to attack when God tries to reach His hand for something you either took or He gave you? Not everything a dog picks up and thinks to eat is good for it. We pick up things and say I will take this, this is good for me. But do you allow our Father to take it if it is not good?

Are you gentle with your words? One of the ways my wife hooked me was because she was gentle and soothing. She can always calm me down and knows what to do to cover me when I am weak.

"Your beauty should not come from outward adornment, such as braided hair and the wearing of gold jewelry and fine clothes. Instead, it should be that of your inner self, the unfading beauty of a gentle and quiet spirit, which is of great worth in God's sight" (1 Peter 3:3-4).

A gentle and quiet spirit has value to God. I know in our society being loud, desiring to be seen with the pictures, and the outlandish outfits have become the norm, but this ought not be so if you have the Fruit of His Spirit which is His command for us. Likewise, Daddy says for us to taste Him to know He is good (Psalms 34:8). We try everything, but will we try and commit to God's way? Will we listen and humble ourselves to know that we are hearing from God and not our lust and desires?

Meekness means to submit, or specifically be submissive to God's Spirit, His way, His commands, His law. His ways are not our ways, because His ways are higher (Isaiah 55:8-9). Yes, the things we must bear and go through may seem impossible, but with God–with His Spirit living on the inside of you–and His Word (Jesus) to back it up all things are possible (Luke 18:27). You are truly more than a conqueror (Romans 8:37) when you are walking in the fruit of the Spirit. We are to be Spiritually led (Romans 8:6) because LIFE is in the spirit not in carnality; carnality leads to death.

We are to walk by faith and not by sight (2 Corinthians 5:7). Lastly, we ought to maintain self-control. It is a virtue to not be ruled by our body, but to be led by our spirit man. We are meant to live inside out, not outside in. In that, your spirit should rule your flesh. Many would say it is natural to do this or that. Why would God give me these urges if they were not to be played out?

God made man to be higher than the beast, animal, fish, and bird because He gave us dominion. He made us slightly lower than angels (Hebrews 2:7 and Psalms 8:5). Yet, He made men (male and female) He created them in His likeness He said in Genesis. We can create, make decisions, and even change our position, unlike angels. When the angels fell from heaven they could never get back.

You are born with a purpose. God wants you to demonstrate His Spirit on earth so you cannot only demonstrate His presence on earth or show you are His son or daughter, but also so you can have dominion. I don't know a prince or a princess that has never had a battle. Royalty must be trained.

They must be practiced in defense, knowledge, and how to conduct themselves before other nations so they can be great ambassadors and rulers of their dominion. To be the greatest in the Kingdom of Heaven, you must serve (Luke 22:26). How can we serve, unless there is a need? God permits things to be as they are, so you may serve one another to demonstrate the Kingdom of God on earth!

How do you follow the voice or commands of God? You have to know His character to ensure you got His voice. Many voices can be heard in your head, but how can you separate them? You must know His Spirit. How can you follow His commands if you don't know them?

The law is a great foundation, but there are over 600 laws written in the Bible. I love what Jesus said to sum it up in Matt 22:37-40, "Jesus said unto him, Thou shalt alove the Lord thy God with all thy bheart, and with all thy soul, and with all thy cmind. This is the first and great commandment. [39] And the second is like unto it, Thou shalt love thy neighbor as thyself. [40] On these two commandments hang all the law and the prophets."

How strong is love? Do you know what LOVE is–not defined by man but by God? Secondly, do you share that LOVE (God) with others? This is the first and great commandment for all believers. To love your neighbor as yourself.

It is amazing to me how people can love everyone else except the man or woman next door to them or in their family. We love the rich, we love the famous, but we hate the brothers and sisters right next door! 1 John 4:20 says, If someone says, "I love God," but hates a fellow believer, that person is a liar; for if we don't love people we can see, how can we love God, whom we cannot see?"

We must be consistent family. We must forgive those that hurt or use us and give them God (LOVE) because they need it. Some will go to the cross battling, but before they die get it right. The thief went to the cross as a thief, but he accepted JESUS when he was hanging and entered paradise! Don't underestimate the power of God!

We follow His commands by being a living example, a living sacrifice which is our reasonable service (Romans 12:1). We don't need to be like Jonah and look down at others–or ourselves and be so quick to say what we don't deserve. Or what God can't do! We have to have crazy faith, to know–and believe all things are possible!

He can take you through your process and bless everyone in your path. People that doubted that His hand was on you will see it–even if it is from afar! He can take you from the poorhouse to the palace.

He is a King and everything belongs to Him. He can give you what you don't deserve and what you didn't work for. Nehemiah got everything gifted to him to rebuild the temple grounds, and didn't pay a dime! Don't give up, hold on; there is more to go!

Keep Your Eyes on Heavenly Things

How can we hold on? Many of us may feel like we are at the ends of our rope! There is no fight left. I am tired, I'm weak Father–but hold on! To hold on, you need something more than words, empty promises, good thoughts, you need power! When you run a marathon or need to take a test in school, they tell you to eat before you come–and the right things.

Food is power to your body. Reading is fundamental for the mind. Joy is the key to happiness. Self-control is necessary to maintain your body. So how are we to keep our eyes on heavenly things, the good food, bread of life?

By rejecting the impulse to follow what is popular in this world. Being like the world is like having a form of godliness but denying the power thereof (2 Timothy 3:5). You know the world would have you out here having two heads, being of two opinions, and then have you justify your dysfunction.

They would tell you that because you have this or that, you can be treated differently. Because I have money in the bank I can slap a person and not go to jail.

Since I am famous I am above the law. Or because of my position within this organization stealing is no longer as big of a deal, but a white-collar crime.

Man is always wanting for there to be a time where he can be used to worship himself. The reason many are out of pocket today with Jesus is because they forget He is with God. Those bitten with the bug of religion love to talk about Jesus the man, but not acknowledge Him in all His power! Let me explain (2 Timothy 3:3-7):

3 But know this, that in the last days perilous times will come: 2 For men will be lovers of themselves, lovers of money, boasters, proud, blasphemers, disobedient to parents, unthankful, unholy, 3 unloving, [b] unforgiving, slanderers, without self-control, brutal, despisers of good, 4 traitors, headstrong, haughty, lovers of pleasure rather than lovers of God,

5 having a form of godliness but denying its power. And from such people turn away! 6 For of this sort are those who creep into households and make captives of gullible women loaded down with sins, led away by various lusts, 7 always learning and never able to come to the knowledge of the truth.

Let's start chewing some of this meat because it is fat on the bone! So perilous times will come. That means full of danger or risk, to an extreme. Wouldn't we all agree it is dangerous to leave your doorstep, drive on the roads, play at the park, eat at a store, date a stranger, and etc? People are flaky, unpredictable, and not stable in their thoughts or actions.

So many people have bought into this doctrine of loving yourself. There is a balance between loving yourself like how God wants you to, and then how the world wants you to. God will tell you to Love yourself and define what Love is. Love is: (1 Cor 13:4-8)

4 Love is patient, love is kind. It does not envy, it does not boast, it is not proud. 5 It does not dishonor others, it is not self-seeking, it is not easily angered, it keeps no record of wrongs. 6 Love does not delight in evil but rejoices with the truth. 7 It always protects, always trusts, always hopes, always perseveres. 8 Love never fails…

Now, look at how we ought to love ourselves and tell me if it is not more identified with the fruits of the Spirit? We are not to love ourselves if it means dishonoring others. You are not narcissistic in worldview, selfish, or have a it is all about me and my feelings mindset. This is not love, this is brat behavior that in our culture has been masquerading as self-love. In the same way, you wouldn't dishonor yourself, you shouldn't dishonor your brother or sister.

When Christ told us to love our neighbor as ourselves, we are to exemplify the fruits of the Spirit within us, to ourselves, and others. This is demonstrating Love or God's character. When we love ourselves in this way we are ministering God to ourselves and those around us. We are living the Kingdom here, which is bringing heaven on earth!

What else is not heaven, being a lover of money!

You cannot love money and God equally. I know many people will tell you, you can get this car, or that house by serving God. From experience, until that car or that house—or whatever you want is put into perspective, you will never get it.

God will not put on you more than you can bear! If you cannot love Him, because you are too busy chasing stuff, he will allow money to depart. It says a fool with money, money will soon depart (Proverbs 21:20).

You will get it but can't keep it. You will buy stuff but can't enjoy it. When the devil gives gifts, they always come with a hangup. But our God gives good gifts, and they add no sorrow!

You know I was thinking, wow! How many people do I know or have heard of that boast, meaning brag? They brag because they are proud of something in their possession or what they have done.

You see them in the music industry showing you chains they don't own. Cars they rented for the photoshoot. They do what we call flex like they got something, or show how they living but their debt is through the roof! They are the ones that believe in something for nothing.

The blasphemy today in music videos is straight appalling–not to mention what we see on tv. It was a time you couldn't curse on tv or radio, you can do these things now. No man would have ever thought of dressing up with a pregnant stomach, because it is out of order. But we got that now! What about the people putting blood in shoes, and just crazy stuff–God sees and will not be mocked! The same way He dealt with wicked kings in the past that encouraged His people to sin, He still can and will do today.

He made King Nebecanezzar eat grass, grow fur, and walk around like an ox chewing the cud for 7 years because he tried Him. We don't need to play with Daddy. I can tell you this, we used to have a generation that feared their parents. We used to run to get into the house before the street light clicked on right?

In this day and age, you can turn the tv on and the parents are crying abuse. They are begging for help from this source, boot camp teachers, or scared straight programs. Kids are out of control, and disobedient to their parents. But these unruly children grow up, and they don't know how to go to school and mind. They fight teachers, fight police, and the list goes on and on.

These same children want expensive phones, technology, clothes, shoes, and when they get them– do you think they know how to treat this stuff? Am I telling you to worship clothes, game systems, toys, or the things we get even as adults? "No," but I think it is about looking at what it cost someone to get this or that for you. How are they showing you Love by getting you something you asked for, or trying to impress you if it is something different. Too many are unthankful for what they get and they don't care if they crush a person's feelings to address it.

People in marriages or these so-called toxic

relationships are dealing with unthankful people too. I ain't talking about myself, maybe not you either, but you know in the world. The people out there, the ones sitting in the back! We live in a society where it is not enough. A man can buy the best ring he can afford, and his soon-to-be bride would get mad about the ring size because of what their girlfriend says or someone they see on tv! But you are not on tv and neither is he. Yall don't have rich people's money either.

You nor that man got the income for what you see on tv, but you want to experience it! We put unrealistic expectations on people because of what others are doing on social media. It is sad how many people in the church want to get and do stuff just to take photos to try and impress someone else that they likely don't even know. This hunger to impress strangers has made us lose sight of a man's heart in this scenario. The people who think like this are unthankful for what they have because they are coveting what someone else has. This is not God's process.

Social media has made another problem rush to the front, unholiness. I remember it used to be a good thing to dress with clothes on. The Big Mama's used to talk about the women that wore skimpy clothes, talked loud, and work at night on corners or strip clubs. It was not a social power move to be a woman in these circles for classy, holy, Christian women.

But I dare you to look at the women in the church. Today–women who have day jobs dress like those in the street and strip club. Too many think how they do and act like them too. They want men that will spend to be with them, and they offer up eye candy, the flesh. But they lack the skills to be a wife–most women today don't or can't cook!

I said it. Come for me, but hear me out because this might bless you! It is time out for living unholy, and that is not just on how you dress, but how you think, move, and have your being. I am not just coming for the ladies, men too! It is time to be holy because God says for you and your wife to be holy because He is. I feel sorry for women out here today with some things I have seen men do to their wives.

What you do behind closed doors matters to God. It is His process that we learn to be sanctified because our bodies are His temple. His Holy Spirit is supposed to live within you! Is it clean, holy, acceptable which is your reasonable service? He just asks you to keep a clean house. But how many of us can't even do that?

Okay, I am going to stop now, I can see the nose flaring up right now. People today, (whispering) women don't like talking about being domestic no more. So we gonna go here, unforgiveness. We live in a cancel culture. Where if you offend me, hurt me, not repeatedly, too many–even kids are saying I give you one time to cross me.

Man if Jesus gave us one time, we would never see the Kingdom, on earth or in heaven! People make mistakes and yes we may get it wrong a few or many times. The chips may fall differently, but we are a working progress. We are imperfect people, trying to get it right. We need each other's patience and not a constant judgment. We are quick to slander someone's name even for what they did in their past, not caring about who they are now. I do think God can overcome anything!

Too many are struggling with self-control. We are out of control. The police, the government, diseases, women, men, children–are simply out of control! We have to reel it in family, or we are going to keep slipping into darkness. You cannot have order where people don't have self-control.

When people are out of control they are quick to anger and are brutal. Road rage, jumping people, bullying folks online, or using words and actions to crush someone's heart or spirit happen every day. For some of us trying to get a loan we get a brutal reality check, we are red-lined out of some activities. We get one time to make a mistake and it is like our credit takes a smackdown!

The system we live in despises good things because to work hard, save, pay your bills, and never mess up is unrealistic. It rains on the just and the unjust. If that is the case, I could be doing everything right and still catch heat. This society expects us to be perfect slaves to the system so we fit into these cookie-cutter profiles–that for most of us just ain't happening!

We can go on and on about how traitors, betrayal, headstrong, and being lovers of pleasure than God has crept into our society, homes, and personal life. Looking at our tv shows alone we can see how a good movie doesn't exist without betrayal. The world will always encourage man to yield into their base natural and ignore their spirit. We must be reminded that the war happening within us, is a war between the spirit and the flesh. Simply put, this war is a fight for how you will live your life.

We can pretend all we want to, to be a tree that is bearing fruit–but these actions are of no use. Do you remember when Jesus was walking and He saw the vibrant, healthy-looking leaves on the fig tree? I want to show you something about that fig tree. You see it was cursed because it had a form of godliness but denied the power. The power would bring forth fruit! When Jesus walked up to the tree after His mouth was good and ready for some figs, this is what happened:

(Mark 11:13-14) 13 And seeing a fig tree afar off having leaves, he came, if haply he might find anything thereon: and when he came to it, he found nothing but leaves; for the time of figs was not yet. 14 And Jesus answered and said unto it, No man eat fruit of thee hereafter forever. And his disciples heard it.

Why was it cursed? It was cursed because it was out of order. Fig tree leaves take the natural course and lose their leaves at the first frost. At the change of season, the leaves may drop, or the plant goes dormant until spring. But for it to be thriving, green, taking nutrients, and bear no fruit, it was not a miracle, but a deceiver.

It was cursed because it was pretending to give fruit, but when you search the pretty leaves, it had nothing to give. No man can eat the leaves, they eat the fruit. So if you have no fruit, you are only drawing people to you for them to admire you, and not the fruit of the Spirit!

Trusting God's Process is keeping your eyes & heart on "heavenly things". What I mean is, looking forward to not only being with Him in heaven but also being with Him now!!!

Jesus told us in Matthew how to pray to the Father, but was any of us really listening?

(Matt 6:9-13) "After this manner, therefore, pray ye: Our Father which art in heaven, Hallowed be thy name. 10 Thy kingdom come, Thy will be done in earth, as it is in heaven. 11 Give us this day our daily bread. 12 And forgive us our debts, as we forgive our debtors. 13 And lead us not into temptation, but deliver us from evil: For thine is the kingdom, and the power, and the glory, forever. Amen."

Do you see why I call Him Daddy? He is our Father, our Holy Daddy, that is seated in heaven. All things should reverence His goodness! His power and His majesty are like a consuming fire. The next verse talks about the Father God's will being done on earth as it is done in heaven. We are to hear His voice and obey His commands. We are to be a product of His kingdom extended to earth!

When you confirm your decision to enact the characteristics of the fruit of the spirit, you will find that you won't stumble nor will you be unfruitful. 2 Peter 1:10 says, "1 Therefore, brethren, be even more diligent to make your call and election sure, for if you do these things you will never stumble." Let us continue…

Renew Your Mind

If you want to win, we know being on God's side is always the winning team! If you want to be productive, fruitful, and successful, you have to go to Him or you won't have rest with whatever you accomplish. When we are in the palm of His hands He is willing to keep us and everything about us–because He purposed it.

I mentioned a short beat ago, that there is a battle for our will–our lifestyle. We all have a natural, carnal, flesh mindset. When we lack self-control, our base nature is in control. Through the fall of man, Adam and Eve sinning in the garden, we are all born into a nature of iniquity (sin). We are now born with a different, perverted nature because of the fall.

If we scroll up a bit in 2 Peter 1:3-4, it says, "As His divine power has given to us all things that pertain to life and godliness, through the knowledge of Him who called us by glory and virtue, by which have been given to us exceedingly great and precious promises, that through these you may be partakers of the divine nature, having escaped the corruption that is in the world through lust."

When we yield ourselves to the fruit of His Spirit, we are allowing ourselves to reconnect to the originally intended nature for men and escape the lust nature that now makes up the base nature. Our natural mindset is rooted in rebellion and not in the obedience of the Father. We are not born with a mindset of serving God, but serving ourselves. No one has to teach babies to be worried about themselves. They know when they get here how to feed themselves. The body knows how to care about the things related to the body.

But the Spirit is kindness, goodness, compassion, love, and etc. These are things the baby needs to learn. The baby learns to share because he/she watches his mother and others they interact with. We learn by seeing and we receive through hearing. So how do we get the fruit of the spirit? How do we get to the point where we want a lifestyle like this? A lifestyle that makes the fruit of His Spirit evident?

'Trusting God's Process As You're Going Through' will give you a renewed mind through the Holy Spirit. When you allow the Holy Spirit to lead your spirit, your body, will, and emotions, you find that you will not stumble. When you lay your life down to God, He is faithful to take good care of you.

He says in the Word, I am going to paraphrase, you know how I do. If I care enough about the birds, to ensure they eat each day why not you? If I care about the grass that is here today and burned up tomorrow, how much more do I care about you? If He does the same thing for the flowers how much more does He care about you?

Of all the things God created, we are the only creation made in His image! You are made lower than angels, but you will judge angels someday! You are–we are important to Daddy and He wants to see us win. This mindset is not one that most of us are born with.

Many of us grew up in sketchy neighborhoods, with wild friends, family members, or a troubled past. We have to renew our mind is erasing everything we ever thought we knew about life and starting over. Paul said I had to count everything I knew as dung! He was a learned man, and still, his education was not sufficient to understand the fundamentals of the Kingdom of God.

Our education doesn't prove nothing to God. He is not impressed with our papers, our accomplishments, nor our riches and assets. He said everything on earth belongs to Him. What do we look like showing Him, His stuff, and saying ooh look at me? We look crazy! He said our best works are like filthy rags to Him, so tell me we don't need the Holy Spirit?

We must have His Spirit so that we can do the impossible. So that we can love people that we don't think we can. Can you imagine what it feels like to be the mother of Emmitt Till? Do you know the pain she must have felt to see her son beaten, bruised, killed in such a brutal way? Yet, she could not take that hatred out on all the people that may have shared the same thoughts, skin color, and locale as the men that did this to her son.

Do you know what would happen if we hated

the people responsible for Jesus' death, who we would have to attack? We would have to attack and hate the church because the church was responsible for Jesus going to the cross! Chew on that for a minute. We can't just sit up comfy in no building. The building turned its back on God when He needed them the most.

Peter denied knowing Jesus three times and cursed. But this was the one that helped them. Showed them mysteries, fed them, talk to them, and talked with them on a regular.

Do you see what we are capable of and why we need a renewed mind? Fear would have us turn our backs on the very one that saved us and is still saving us today! We owe Jesus everything, and He is asking us to trust Him with our hearts and our minds so that we can do the will of the Father. But for too many of us, we act like that is too much!

He ain't asking us to go to the cross, He might ask us to stay up and pray. Many of us will scroll through IG, watch movies, or talk on the phone instead. Or we are guilty of doing what the other disciples did and fall asleep.

Be encouraged, our Father can renew our minds and set us on the right path so that we may understand things that otherwise we couldn't. Jesus said (Matt 13:10-12), "Then the disciples came to Jesus and asked, "Why do You speak to the people in parables?" He replied, "The knowledge of the mysteries of the kingdom of heaven has been given to you, but not to them.

Whoever has will be given more, and he will have an abundance. Whoever does not have, even what he has will be taken away from him."

The mysteries that are hard to understand through parables can be understood, when you renew your mind and live out the principles for the fruit of the Spirit and simply be led by God. To make it through life, we have to make it through the process of life. In going through life, how much better can we live when we Trust God through that process. Allowing Him to renew our minds, and show us how things were and will be, we must submit ourselves to God and be led by His Spirit.

This is the secret to the Kingdom of heaven and another truth like it, we must keep our minds on good things. Philippians 4:8 says, "Finally, brethren, whatsoever things are true, whatsoever things are honest, whatsoever things are just, whatsoever things are pure, whatsoever things are lovely, whatsoever things are of good report, if there be any virtue and if there be any praise, think on these things."

As we keep our minds set on the things that are good, honest, true, and pure we find ourselves eating and feeding our mind, soul, body, and spirit with it! Whatever you watch, listen to, or consume by any means is shaping your thoughts, ideas, and lifestyle. It is critical that we renew our minds by meditating on the Word, its truth, ideas, and practices day and night.

So, simply put, I am sure you know it doesn't mean just reading your Bible all day and thinking about it. Many of us work, have jobs, raise children, have spouses, and etc. However, in all these things we do regularly, we should be thinking of ways to incorporate kingdom principles into that situation. The more we meditate and engage the Word in our thoughts, ideas, and perceptions, the more we are empowered to live a kingdom life.

Romans 12:2, "Do not conform to the pattern of this world, but be transformed by the renewing of your mind. Then you will be able to test and approve what God's will is—his good, pleasing and perfect will." I often have to reflect and reassess my mind. Am I thinking of things that edify God or something else? Do I spend time focusing on how to be more like Him or being conformed to this world? I wrote this piece based on the relationship I have with God and how I wanted Him to soften my heart towards Him.

Again, I wasn't always open to God, but when I made the decision that I wanted a relationship with Him I needed Him to soften my heart and open my mind to His word. If you want to build that relationship with Him, ask Him to do it for you. You cannot live this life, nor be led by His Spirit without a relationship with Him.

Original journal entry, entitled, "RELATIONSHIP!"

Family, this is Thursday night, Nissan 13th. It's Passover, it's Jesus' final Passover celebration. As a matter of fact, this is Jesus' 53rd step He's making in his earthly journey.

Ok, let me tell you real fast, there were 72 steps

or recorded segments of Jesus' life. He descended from heaven, to be born of a young virgin girl. From Glory to Bethlehem (Lk 2:1-21) and to The Mt. of Olives where Jesus departed for home (Mk 16:19,20-Acts 1:4-11). Holy Spirit, please lead as You will…

His love desired a reconciled 'Relationship' with us. He did it all to get us back!!! Imma start at step #10…After John the Baptist baptized Jesus, the heavens opened up & GOD THE FATHER spoke as GOD THE HOLY SPIRIT sat upon GOD THE SON & made it known not just here on the earth, but in all the universe that "THIS (JESUS) IS MY BELOVED SON IN WHOM I AM WELL PLEASED!!!" (Matt 3:17)

From that point until we get to John 15:9-12, Jesus has had these 12 dudes hanging out with Him, eating, sleeping, laughing, listening, and watching everything that He did. They witnessed the thousands of miracles that He performed, though the script only records 38 or so. But (read John 21:25) yes, there were so many things that The Lord had done, that the world can not contain them all if they were all written.

Yeah, it's so much that these men had experienced with Jesus. From their vantage point, they've actually seen how God Himself deals with imperfect people with attitudes, who are grumpy, lying, or a thief, sneaky, passive, selfish, even cussing homeboys'. And yet, Jesus loved them even after seeing their imperfection–and He loved them enough to give His life to redeem them. He loves us all the same!!!

Ok, as I mentioned earlier, it's Passover. They

just finished celebrating the meal with one another and of course, Jesus is reminding them of their experiences and the importance of staying in RELATIONSHIP with Him!!! Going back to verse 1 of this chapter, Jesus tells them of His relationship with God the Father. Jesus told them that He is the true vine & that DADDY was the husbandman.

He also said how God is the gardener who cares for the vine, the branch, and that fruit will be plentiful coming from it. From verses 1-11, The Lord Jesus helps them to appreciate having a relationship with God. Jesus told us to "abide," which means to dwell, to be close, or in a place that's with The Father. This is the point of abiding in God; it means to have true love for one another.

Fam, the world doesn't like any of us because the world doesn't like the Father's principles. As a matter of fact, we're hated by the world!!! Now, hate is having a strong dislike for or hostility (a warlike aggression) towards something. The world has animosity, despises, scorns, and is unloving toward godly truth.

So don't be confused because we work alongside folks, and hap'nd 2 live next door that they love you. People can be cordial, kind, and be the best person you met so far, but they still may not like the God in you. It should be our heart's and mind's desire to develop the heart of Christ towards God, 1 another, and have that same love for the lost souls that may hate His principles at the time of us meeting them.

Jesus said, that there's "no greater love hath no

man that he will die 4 his friends". I'm jack'd up and I got humungous issues in some areas, but I'm in love with Christ. U Kno' I got issues, but my heart is truly 4 Jesus. I do exemplify the fruit of the Spirit as often as I can, and my shortcomings are nowhere near what they used to be. But with all the good I have done, Who would give up their life 4 me?? I'm Ur Brutha we may say, but many of us will not lay our lives down for each other. But those that have a relationship with God, can do it!

In the beginning of man's existence, Jehovah God had a relationship with us. Gen 2:7 doesn't speak of man's birthday until the 11 verse and after that, The LORD mentioned that it is not good for man to be alone. Adam was spend'n lots of time with God, this time was building a relationship! Adam was alone because there was no one like him. Relationship, again is what our Father desires of us. For He and us to be on one accord-or in agreement.

Idk why I was directed to write this during my prayer time today. Maybe it's because of me… Perhaps I need 2 reassess myself, my relationship with The Father, my family, and my brethren. Our relationship with God does shape the relationship we can have with humanity and any other bond. I do love each & every one of y'all in the body of Christ & ain't nuth'n u can do about it!!!

The scripture says, "Ask and it shall be given you… Seek and ye shall find… Knock and it shall be opened unto you… For every one that asketh, receiveth and he that seeketh findeth and to him that knocketh it shall be opened" (Matt7:7,8). It's just that simple, just ask Him. But, I don't want to use the word 'but' here, though it's absolutely necessary to do so. Just asking because your mouth & tongue can formulate the correct words together, but with no belief in what you are asking for will yield no results.

Many folks do & say things because they've been instructed to do so. They can perform the task because it's 'ritualistic' and out of habit. Two other reasons are feeling obligation or because they want to be compensated and rewarded in some way. Now, Jesus says to two blind men one day, "Believe ye that I'm able to do this?" (Matt 9:28-b). Belief & trust go hand-in-hand. To trust is to have or place confidence in, to depend on, to give credibility to, or to believe. To believe is to have faith, confidence, or trust, to expect or suppose & to be convinced of that truth.

Now, I bring this up to make a quick solid point; You may ask The LORD, to allow you to draw close to Him, to trust Him. But if you don't believe that He can do what you're asking of Him, He won't do it. Remember what I just said about Jesus asking the two blind men, do they believe He could heal them? Notice the next verse: "Then He (Jesus) touched his eyes, saying, 'according to your faith' be it unto you"!! (Matt 9:29). It was up to the men to see after the men came to Jesus for help (Matt 9:27).

Persevere and Never Turn Back!

Trusting God's Process entails believing in His Word and trusting what He says concerning you and to you. This faith that builds out of the confidence you have in God will empower you to persevere under trials. I said earlier how many saints right now are battling many things today. We are going through a test on every side, "We are hard-pressed on all sides, but not crushed; perplexed, but not in despair; persecuted, but not forsaken; struck down, but not destroyed" (2 Corinthians 4:8-10).

Even though He may slay us, still we must decide if we will trust God like Job (Job 15:13). There is always an intended end for anything we endure. The hard things or the light, all work for the good of those that love God and are called according to His purpose (Romans 8:28).

The fruits of the Spirit tell us not to render evil for evil, because what is the reward in that? But to suffer for righteousness' sake, do we inherit a prize. In 1 Peter 3:14-18 Jesus describes the blessings we acquire for persevering through a trial–if we suffer for righteousness' sake.

14 But and if ye suffer for righteousness sake, happy are ye: and be not afraid of their terror, neither be troubled; 15 But sanctify the Lord God in your hearts: and be ready always to give an answer to every man that asketh you a reason of the hope that is in you with meekness and fear: 16 Having a good conscience; that, whereas they speak evil of you, as of evildoers, they may be ashamed that falsely accuse your good conversation in Christ. 17 For it is better, if the will of God be so, that ye suffer for well-doing than for evil doing. 18 For Christ also hath once suffered for sins, the just for the unjust, that he might bring us to God, being put to death in the flesh, but quickened by the Spirit:

When we endure we are acting and demonstrating the love that Jesus defined. If we suffer for evil-doing, it is payment, but if we suffer for righteousness' sake, it is a divine sacrifice, holy, and acceptable by God because this act is by faith. We ought to live by faith because without faith, we cannot please God (2 Corinthians 5:7, Hebrews 11:16).

Our faith is built by trusting God, and that confidence is established with the help of the Holy Ghost. He speaks to us and tells us all things. The Holy Spirit wants to lead and guide us, He also comforts us in times of uncertainty or despair. This is the Spirit that indwelled in Jesus all the days He was on earth. This Spirit, His Spirit, was then poured out so that it may dwell with all who would receive Him into their temple (body).

Jesus said in John 14:26, "But the Comforter, which is the Holy Ghost, whom the Father will send in my name, he shall teach you all things, and bring all things to your remembrance, whatsoever I have said unto you." We are empowered by what Jesus did for us and continues to do inside of us through the work of the Holy Spirit. When we allow the Holy Spirit to revive our spirit and keep us, by dwelling within us, we will have victory over everything.

It is the Holy Spirit that helps us to live out the fruits of the Spirit because these are His gifts. He knows how they work and how to remind you to use them. When we go through it is imperative that we watch what we say, how we think, and what we do. Do you know that your greatest witness is not what you say but how you live?

People watch how and what you suffer. They want to know if knowing God really makes a difference in someone's life. Does encountering God have a tangible, visual implication, or is it all in a person's head? If a person is truly born of the Spirit, they must exemplify His characteristics. We would say that you are your father's child if there are similarities in how you look, talk, walk, DNA, blood, etc with your proposed father.

The same can be likened to the children of God. To be like Him we must also pick up His traits, likeness, holiness, fruits of the Spirit, and do them. As we become more like God, we find that we start to lean more into our renewed minds. This renewed mind is necessary for us to advance to the next step of the process, perseverance.

It is hard to go through a trial if you have not yet made your election sure. Making your election sure, is making a decision, or making up your mind about how you think and believe. 2 Peter 1: 10 says, "Therefore, brothers, strive to make your calling and election sure. For if you practice these things you will never stumble."

Knowing that your mind is made up, you are not a double-minded man or woman unstable in your ways (James 1:8). You have made a decision and you are sticking to it. This decision gives you roots, so when the wind of trials blow your way, you will be able to stand. When life happens, you won't allow the trial to put you in doubt. You must know your calling so that you can be sure of your election–decision.

Every man and woman on earth has a purpose, and it is our job to understand the will of God for our lives. If you are called to be married, you may have to persevere through some tests an unmarried person may not have to. You may have arguments, life lessons, financial growth, and other issues you have to work through.

When you select a wife if you are a man, or a husband if you are a woman, you decided to be in a relationship with someone. You then have decided to make this union recognized by God when you married publicly. Your friends and family who were present for the celebration, should keep you both in remembrance of your calling to be a husband or a wife, and hold you accountable for the decision you both made when you want to quit.

Too often we are not driven to persevere when things get tough, we want to jump out the window, run out the door, quit, or just fall out! We don't want to go through the pain, dysfunction, embarrassment, or shame, we just want the good stuff. The happy endings, the good times, and pleasant things. But I tell you, every relationship, problem, or situation if you are a believer is designed to make you more like Christ.

The wife or husband you picked, because you felt the calling to be married, didn't change because your flesh doesn't like this or that. Or because there is some trouble in paradise. We must put away selfish ways of thinking and understand Jesus' way of living.

In Philippians 3:10-21 is the following passage: "That I may know him, and the power of his resurrection, and the fellowship of his sufferings, being made conformable unto his death; If by any means I might attain unto the resurrection of the dead. Not as though I had already attained, either were already perfect: but I follow after, if that I may apprehend that for which also I am apprehended of Christ Jesus. Brethren, I count not myself to have apprehended: but this one thing I do, forgetting those things which are behind, and reaching forth unto those things which are before, I press toward the mark for the prize of the high calling of God in Christ Jesus.

Let us, therefore, as many as be perfect, be thus minded: and if in anything ye be otherwise minded, God shall reveal even this unto you. Nevertheless, whereto we have already attained, let us walk by the same rule, let us mind the same thing. Brethren, be followers together of me, and mark them which walk so as ye have us for an example.

For many walk, of whom I have told you often, and now tell you even weeping, that they are the enemies of the cross of Christ: Whose end is destruction, whose God is their belly, and whose glory is in their shame, who mind earthly things. For our conversation is in heaven; from whence also we look for the Saviour, the Lord Jesus Christ: Who shall change our vile body, that it may be fashioned like unto his glorious body, according to the working whereby he is able even to subdue all things unto himself."

When we subject our body and mind to the leadership of the Holy Spirit, He will help us to deny ourselves. The flesh has a built-in survival mechanism. No one has to teach us how to fight to live, we naturally do it. In caring, loving, and showing the fruits of the Spirit, we learn to not be selfish, and narcissistic. By treating others in this fashion we are doing what Christ would have us to. We must love our wives as Christ loves the church (Ephesians 5:25). Women are to respect their husbands (Ephesians 5:33).

These two things are not as hard to do with the Holy Spirit guiding you. I cannot imagine the struggle without His help! It is easy to fall into what I deserve and talk yourself out of a relationship, but if you do that, you are quitting the assignment. You are not learning to persevere but to run away. You are not learning to endure, but to escape. Our generation loves "get out of jail free cards," but these cards don't usually teach us anything. Many of us mistake not being judged for being okay.

When we live like this we abuse the Grace of God and use it as a weapon against God. We have not been set free from the law, so we can then use grace to sin. We must instead, learn from our mistakes and encourage ourselves to persevere. We persevere by believing this pain shall pass. Can you imagine if a woman only had the memory of childbirth on her mind, could she ever see herself having more children?

When women go through childbirth and then see the baby growing up, most of them think about wanting or having another child. Some people say she is crazy to go through that kind of pain the first time–then to think she wants more than one, two, or three seems insane! But if we only focus on that hard day, we will never see the many more good days that follow. We will never get to the celebration of 30 years, 40 years, and 50 years of marriage if we focus on the hard days only!

Too many are settling for one-year engagements, 5-year marriages, and broken families that continuously start over and never become stable. This is not limited to just marriage, but also personal growth, starting a business, or advancing on the job. If you are trying to do something new, and you keep getting knocked down, do you quit?

Did you work real hard for a promotion and when you are overlooked, you stop trying from that day forward to advance? Do you let one "no," or several "no's" stop you from getting a "yes?" I know it is hard to get up and go to work for a company when you don't feel like you are appreciated. I know it is not easy to stay in a position you feel is under your pay grade or experience, but can you push through it if you must?

I remember I had to take any job I could get to keep the lights on. I was willing to work for everything I had, which was hard, because when you are used to money coming easy–it's humbling for that to change. When you are used to making a $100 in an hour, and now it takes you a half or full day to get there. You may feel it in your spirit to quit but don't.

When we persevere through trials we are learning ourselves, but most importantly God. God is a patient God. He believes in longsuffering, and I know this isn't popular. We live in a society of cancel culture thinkers. If something doesn't rub us the right way, look right, talk right, or act right, we want to cancel them from our lives. But this isn't relationship family. Family is meant to push your buttons and challenge you.

Can you imagine how it must have felt for Jesus to travel through many countries healing, teaching, and performing miracles all to be regarded among His hometown as a common carpenter–or as one of Mary's children? The people that knew Him before He started His ministry, I believe knew He was different, but they struggled with accepting His greatness. They saw Him work through trials, challenges, and persevere, but they were not convinced He could be more than what they saw Him do growing up. Family is some of the hardest people to win over, aren't they?

But if you can get your family on the same page,

wow! What can be the result? One person can put a 1,000 to flight but two 10,000. This math doesn't compute the same. This is why it is so important to treat people right, be patient, allow people to grow, and even change. Because Jesus plus any person is more than enough to impact the world. We cannot limit ourselves or each other, based on what we must go through, endure, or persevere through.

There is a reason for our suffering and a reward for when we endure. I would even argue we have a reward in this life and the one to come! Our marriages win because we stay married and allow the marriage to finish a work that was started in us.

Our family benefits, because had it not been for my mother believing in me, I don't think I would have had the heart or mind to get it right. Even on her deathbed, unknown to her, she believed in me persevering through my test. She never gave up on me and if we don't give up on each other and most importantly God, we will have a reward!

2 Timothy 4:7-8 says, "I have fought a good fight, I have finished my course, I have kept the faith: Henceforth there is laid up for me a crown of righteousness, which the Lord, the righteous judge, shall give me at that day: and not to me only, but unto all them also that love his appearing.

Persevering through trials not only blesses the people going through the test but those watching it. People that see you come out on the other side will ask you someday, how did you do it? How did you stay on the job after this or that happened? How do you believe in your new business even when things looked bad? How did you stay married so long with life's challenges?

Persevering blesses the next generation. Those that endure are the saints that refuse to be like folks who don't know or love God. Because we know what God has done for us, it humbles us and allows us to be slow to speak at times. Longsuffering when we need to be. Patient when it is required, gentle, loving, kind, self-controlled, and etc.

Trusting God's Process As You Go Through, will help you to endure persecution, perform mighty acts of righteousness, and suffer for God. As we keep our hearts right toward God and are committed to persevering for righteousness' sake, it makes us stronger in God too! This strength empowers us NOT to GIVE UP & RETURN BACK TO THE OLD LIFE That WE CAME OUT FROM because we know His power and ability to take us through any test or trial.

Our election is made sure, and our heart is set on keeping our commitment to God. We desire to be a faithful servant and to put Him above all other things. We make Him the King and Lord of our life, and we will follow Him until the day we die, come hell or high water as the Big Momma's used to say.

We know that the benefits are receiving a crown, inheriting placement in an eternal kingdom, and having confidence that all things work to our good when we persevere, but what would happen if we choose to not trust God? What if we decided to do things our way?

The Penalty of Doing Things Your Way

It will always be tempting to lean on our own thoughts, emotions, feelings, and experience. We are instructed not to lean on our understanding of things, because that can lead us in the wrong direction. A lot of people are like adult children, in fact Daddy says we ought to be like little children so we don't miss the kingdom. If we are to be like little children, we should listen to our heavenly parent, God the Father, so that we know how to live.

The Bible says to obey your mother and father so that your days may be long (Exodus 20:12). Why are we instructed to follow our parents, so that our days may be long? Likely, because your parents know more–especially when their children are younger. Parents have experiences and wisdom that trumps feelings and emotions. These experiences build reactions, responses, and help shape decisions that could help others if they would only listen.

Ephesians 6:1-3 also says, "Children, obey your parents in the Lord, for this is right. "Honor your father and mother"—which is the first commandment with a promise— "so that it may go well with you and that you may enjoy long life on the earth." Again, we are told the same thing in the Old and New Testament. The biggest question we must ask ourselves is why? Why would God tell us not once but twice the same thing? Hmmm, I am thinking because it matters–and it matters a lot!

If we don't learn to regard or respect authority, we will struggle in all the other areas of our lives. Respecting our parents is part of the ten commandments given to Moses and we know that these were given to the Hebrews after they left Egypt. These laws and commands were set so the people would know how to live.

As believers, we cannot live life any way we want to. We read in Galatians 5:17, "For the flesh desires what is contrary to the Spirit, and the Spirit what is contrary to the flesh. They are in conflict with each other, so that you are not to do whatever you want."

There is a way we are expected to live and if we break this command, we must be prepared to deal with the consequences. If you do not regard authority first in the natural, you would also likely, not regard spiritual authority in the spiritual realm. When Jesus came to earth, the Jews wanted a King for the here and now. They were not concerned about spiritual matters, but about wealth, prestige, status, and rulership over the earth. They wanted to be put back in power, and be the ruling power again instead of the underlings of society.

Jesus told the Jews why He came and what He purposed to do, but they were carnally minded and could not perceive what He was saying and doing. As it is written in Mark 4:11-12, "And he said unto them,

Unto you it is given to know the mystery of the kingdom of God: but unto them that are without, all these things are done in parables: That seeing they may see, and not perceive; and hearing they may hear, and not understand..."

Jesus spoke in parables so that people would not understand even though they heard His words. People can read this Bible, but if they don't have the Holy Spirit, because they chose not to yield their spirit, they will not understand the Bible fully as intended. We can know something in part and so when we speak or do something it may not yield the intended fruit (1 Corinthians 13:9). If you get half of a story, how many mistakes will you likely make? Possibly a lot!

When we didn't want kids in grown folk conversations, what did we do? I remember Big Momma and my mother would start spelling stuff. I felt like I was in a spelling bee sometimes when trying to keep up with their conversation. I remember before I got saved when people preached to me, it would go in one ear and out the other. I was hearing, but I was not understanding. I was seeing people living holy, but I didn't either believe or allowed my thinking to downplay the results.

You know that if you see a good thing happening, you would say something like, "It only worked because they got money. Or they look good. Talk well, or whatever?" We always got an excuse for why people win or fail, but it is usually based on carnal things. We don't see the demons that come and dwell with us when we refuse to follow God's order and process.

So in short, if you skip His process, you will be blind to the things of the spirit and you will lack discernment as a result. Many people walking around right now don't know what is wrong with them. They think it is everything else, but the truth is demons are real. Spiritual warfare is real family. If we don't have eyes to see and perceive what is happening in our lives, we will give the devil dominion over things we should be taking authority over.

Let me explain this real quick, because I know I just said a mouthful. You see, as we have talked about earlier, you know that you are living by His Spirit when you exemplify the fruit of the Spirit. Review chapter 6 for more on that, but if you are choosing to skip the process of submitting to the Holy Spirit, and electing to lean on your knowledge you will have some problems. 2 Peter 3:9 says, "For he who lacks these things is shortsighted, even to blindness, and has forgotten that he was cleansed from his old sins."

The danger of leaning on your own understanding is you will go back to what you used to be. When we lose the care, and understanding of what Jesus delivered us from, we forget about our sins. As soon as we forget about our sins, we are just as quick to return to our old vomit (Proverbs 26:11). I know we look at dogs when they do this and say, "Stupid dog. Why are you going back and eating that? Don't you know that just made you sick?"

This is the penalty for skipping God's process. You will go back to whatever and however, you used to be. Sometimes when you go back you are way worst than you were the first time. You go from bad to good, to worst. It's a sad thing to see the hard work people do, all to go back to the streets, drinking, drugs, addictions, lying, stealing, cheating, or whatever was their issue.

If we don't submit ourselves to God when He fixes our life we will run up on what we got delivered from. When we are ungrateful for the work of the Holy Spirit in our lives, we run the risk to grieve the Holy Spirit. The Bible tells us not to grieve the Holy Spirit (Ephesians 4:30). Yes, we can make the Holy Spirit mad, or upset, and we can push Him away from us with our actions. We must accept the Holy Spirit in our lives and make room for Him. We cannot assume after we have been delivered in a church service that, that was all we had to do!

Matthew 12:43-45 says, " When the unclean spirit is gone out of a man, he walketh through dry places, seeking rest, and findeth none." If a demon is cast out, it goes out and looks for a new home. If it cannot live among anyone near you, it will go away not to leave you alone, but to go and get stronger. If you are not careful, you subject everyone around you to danger.

The seven sons of Sceva were messed up by demons because they didn't have the Holy Spirit, power, to fight the enemy. When the demons left a man they tortured them. The demons showed the men that they didn't know Jesus nor the Holy power He and Paul had. When they tried to use that power out of their carnality, it backfired!

Likewise, if we try to fight a spiritual problem

with carnal answers, nothing will happen that will end well. I will never take people into a room to cast out a demon or demonic spirit that doesn't truly know God. To bring people into a room that lacks faith, belief, and power, is to open them up to more demon problems. Why do you think Jesus kicked people out of rooms before he cast out spirits? Death is a spirit? Sickness, disease, and I can go on and on. We must fight a spiritual attack in the spirit.

Verse 44 says, "Then he saith, I will return into my house from whence I came out; and when he is come, he findeth it empty, swept, and garnished." When we get delivered and forgiven, God separates our sins as far as the east is from the west (Psalm 103:12). He cast our sins into the sea of forgetfulness and makes us as white as snow (Micah 7:19, Isaiah 1:18).

Have you ever seen how children and busybodies love to mess up a clean house? They don't mind living in junk, but if you clean everything, it is like you gave them new wind to run around and mess some stuff up. You have to make them sit down so they don't drive you crazy.

I use children not because they are bad, but because we are like children, rebellious and unruly until we mature in God's process. Your age doesn't signify growth, but the fruit of the spirit does. So I say family, where is your fruit? If you don't have the Spirit present, that demon coming back because the house is clean and ain't nobody there.

If you were a thief and a robber, or a hobo with

no house. You may choose to lay up like a squatter for as long as you can. A squatter will use your power, water, and even trash your place. They don't mind tearing up your place because they don't own it.

Demons are just like this, they squat in your body and wreak havoc on your life. They don't care about you because, at the end of the day, they don't own it. They let you pay the penalty of sin and death and they enjoy seeing you brought down to their level.

Squatters don't mind seeing people suffer from their actions, they laugh about it. They are heartless, ruthless, and could care less about who is affected because of their misfortune. We all got a story for why we don't have, end up homeless, and the demons got one too!

The last verse 45 says, "Then goeth he, and taketh with himself seven other spirits more wicked than himself, and they enter in and dwell there: and the last state of that man is worse than the first. Even so, shall it be also unto this wicked generation." This is like people turning your house into a trap house, a den of thieves, or a place where illegal things you shouldn't approve happen.

We are not the author of sin, the devil is and so are the fallen angels. They are operating illegally in the spirit realm, and we have to call them on it. The only thing, in order to have jurisdiction on making them leave and stay gone, you have to have the Holy Spirit.

We just learned you cannot come and kick them

out without no power! If you come into your house and drug dealers, gang bangers, or whatever is living up in there, you ain't gone kick them out because you ask nicely. They gon laugh in your face! They probably going to clown you if they don't beat you up. Are you seeing what happened to the sons of Sceva?

They asked demons nicely to live, but the Bible tells us in Matthew 11:12 that, "From the days of John the Baptist until now the kingdom of heaven suffers violence, and violent men take it by force." We are on a battlefield and we are battling for dominion. We are fighting for victory over our mind, body, will, and emotions! This battle has to be taken by force! You need power! Without Holy Ghost power, you will lose!

If we skip the process we will lose the battle and the war. There is nothing gained from skipping God's process except failure. If you skip a test here, you can't go to the next grade and expect to succeed. You don't know the material from the previous grade. You will fail. God is not a God that will pass you on to not hurt your feelings.

He says He sent His Son to divide and put people at odds over truth! There is only one truth. One God and one Baptism. There are not many ways to God it is only one way. God's process is the only way to get through to heaven.

There is no way around it, and we have to trust God as we go through. To go against His truth, refuse His love, power, and influence, leaves you naked as we were in the garden. You are open, prey for the lions to come and devour.

I like this journal entry I wrote that I think is necessary to share with you at this moment:

Original journal entry, entitled "Change"

Change… As we all become aware seems almost impossible for it to be. When things arise from you, it is possible for you not to know how it developed inside of you. That's a real sobering thought, 'scary' even to the point where I (we) can be paralyzed by it. It can anger me to find a thing or things inside of me that I can't control or dismiss totally.

What are some of the things that come up from deep within? How did those things get there we may ask ourselves when it shows up. Are they from experiences or are they inherited? Are they 'spells' cast upon us from generations ago or a result of our choices? What about changes that are self-inflicted? Can I just 'pray' it away or 'wish' it off of me? Can I say, as I have said a ga-zillion, qua'trillion times before, "I'm not doing that again," or "I'm not gonna think like that, say that, feel that again!!" LORD, you know my heart & I wanna please you. Yeah, you know, that conversation, over & over that happens or maybe it is just me?

My prayer often is, "change me, LORD!!" I… "I don't want to be this way. I submit myself to You, Daddy… I am tired of this thought process of "foolishness." LORD, you have my permission to change me for Your Glory & for Your Honour. I'm not qualified to represent You in any sort of way… I can't even claim You, Jesus, without You directing me & You allowing me to do so. My heart hurts Daddy when I think of my shortcomings, but I am open to the change! When I do or say anything that's going to bring dishonor to You, I don't rest easy. As I'm writing this, my eyes are full of tears & my heart is hurting.

LORD, please forgive me. I'm so sorry for not being able to love You, as You deserve to be loved and as I want to love you. I thank You because I know you are good to me. Holy Ghost, thank you for directing me. Father, I need you to continue to change my heart, mind, body, and soul. I thank You, Father, that You keep loving on me & allowing me to truly have love, great desire–& passion to love You fully!!" Yeah, this is one of my 'it just came up' daily conversations' with Daddy!!

I'm going to tell you, I'm frightened that their are things I struggle with. I am not a perfect man, but I am trying to be made perfect. I am frightened about the 'pain of change'. It hurts me to see & realize that some things on my own I can't change even though I wanted to! But Daddy saved me and I want to show Him how much I've changed, but I still need His help to continue changing.

The Apostle Paul said in Rom 7:19 "For the good that I would I do not: but the evil which I would not, that I do."

So, how do or can I change if I am stuck? How am I to be "used of God" with 'that other side of me' always pushing its way to the forefront? Oh, how about when you're fasting, praying & you know The LORD heard you but you are waiting. You kno' your conversation with Him is acceptable, that your heart is held in His hands, but you haven't received the 'breakthrough.' No 'releasing of it' has happened yet and you so desperately need change. The change is well, it's not there yet?

What happens you feel discouragement or are accused of being a thief but you are not. When accused of being a liar but you are not. You don't cuss in your speech, or haven't cuss'd anyone out recently but you are being pressed. You're a helper to your family, the brethren in the church, and your community. You encourage others or try when every opportunity comes their way. You are now a kind person, forgiving, you "gave up ur guns" (war mentality) by choice. Today, you "won't bust a grape, in a fruit fight". You have been changed, and you are waiting on a change to come.

Now, please understand me, I'm truly not complaining. I know that through Christ, 'all things are possible.' I have seen the change in me. I am living because of 'the change' in my life. From a little guy, to a preteen, from a teenager until adulthood I have changed! Growing into 'a full-grown man' I see the change. Not just in the physical, but the emotional, the mental & since Jesus, the spiritual… I never actually thought, or realized how change was at play. Most importantly, I never knew how God was always "in the mix!!" and changing things.

I remember actually when I started walking… I was 8 months old. Some say that you can't remember that far back because they can't remember that far back!! I remember starting pre-K at 3 ½ yrs old. My early memory is strong and I went from joy to anger. From fear to insanity. From being hopeful to being devastated. From whoring like a madman to being the 'dope-man', then to becoming the dope-phen'. I was shot up 3xs, pronounced deceased 2xs, toe tag 2xs. Put in prison, homeless… yes, they were all my experiences. I've had some good times, scary times, and honestly bad times. I wasn't sure at the moment what it was, but my life changed. I traveled from "a course of death, to a pathway of life"…

Prayer, trust, faith then doing what God's will is for me (Garry). My change is daily. There must be a renewal of my ever-growing love for Christ, for His company (His indwelling). I always want Him to lead me where He says for me to go. One thing that I may say that's in my favor, I believe… is that I do love God's Word!!! That has put the 'seal', 'the icing on the cake', so to speak for me. Yeah, it has & still is sustaining me to this day!!

My constant 'molding', regardless of the "jet-eye mind game" of my sinful nature, has me continually reminded of Col 3:10-17 and especially verses 16-17. These verses say, "Letting the Word of Christ dwell in you (me) richly in all wisdom. Whatever ye do in word or deed, do it in Jesus' name, giving thanks to God."

I'm truly thankful, yeah, I'm truly grateful to God for 'change'. I recognize we serve a "progressive God". He is constantly going forth to complete us. I also recognize that without this foundation, I absolutely, positively couldn't make it!! With this, I'm able to submit myself & allow the Holy Spirit to guide me.

Although at times I'm uncertain of the "change", yet, I'm willing to go through for the sake of growing. For me to have a 'true relationship' with Jesus, I must invite "the change." This change is always for God's Glory.... And Garry's benefit. Thank you, God!

>Garry Washington

A Conclusion on The Matter

Now, at this exact point of me jotting this down on paper, as I mentioned earlier, I've been 'through the fire.' My body started acting like it was being tortured. Some people at my job started acting up. Bills started to pile up on me. I have been evicted, lost employment before, spent some time in jail, been pronounced dead twice, and even had a toe tag twice! I was out of here but GOD! Some people don't understand my praise because they don't know my story.

I wanted to tell you my story, so when you see me shouting you have a glimpse as to why. When you see me crying, it is not because I am overly emotional for no reason–but because I show my gratitude all the day long. When I know I should be dead, because I was dead! I have to dance and thank Him! I cannot summarize this book without giving God, my Heavenly Father, my Daddy thanks! He took me in as His son and has been so patient with me.

I have done many things wrong, but family I got this part right. I know for you to ever have something you have to be down during the good and bad times. One thing I learned from growing up in the streets–like many of us, we are all looking to find someone who will be down for us through thick or thin. We want unconditional love, loyalty, and someone that will always come through!

I tell you, I have searched far and wide, high and low, and only one can fit the bill. God! He is the only one that has proven to be faithful even when I wasn't faithful–when you are not faithful. He will be there with you and stand with you in good and bad times. He will not lead you astray nor is He trying to bait you into a dark alley to jump you for your shoes. He owns everything in heaven and below it!

He knows the number of hairs on your head. He cares for you and about you. He has gone to great lengths to keep you. Do you know Jesus has an assignment to keep all of God's children on the right path? John 17:12 says, "While I was with them in the world, I kept them in thy name: those that thou gavest me I have kept, and none of them is lost, but the son of perdition; that the scripture might be fulfilled. "

Yes, Jesus has a special assignment to hold our hands and show us the right way to go through the process. He was not only willing to tell us the way but to live it. He came from heaven to earth, took on flesh, and suffered for us. He died and was crucified to ensure we had a process to living a Kingdom lifestyle. There is a lot of moving parts to God's process.

It is He that sits at the head of the table and looks down from heaven on His children. He gave us the Word, that was brought to earth by way of the Holy

Spirit (Ghost) and a virgin woman. The Word took on flesh, so that He may endure all things and prove what is possible when the Holy Spirit lives on the inside of us!

Jesus was born with God's Spirit and when He died, resurrected, and after He ascended to heaven, he told the disciples to be patient because I have a gift for you! They had to wait on the gift. They didn't know when it was coming, but they were sure it would. When they were in the upper room a mighty wind blew through the place and the Holy Spirit was poured out into the world so that all who would believe in the Lord Jesus Christ and accept the Spirit of God (the Holy Spirit/Ghost) to live within them would operate in power!

Jesus didn't release the Spirit so that we can just say we got it or believe He exists. He did it so that greater works can be done because all the children of God now can have His Spirit living on the inside of them. Instead of just indwelling one man, He can indwell within mankind again as before. We are no longer cut off from God but connected through His Spirit! When we are connected to His Spirit, we will bear the evidence when we have the fruit of the spirit.

We can be kind, patient, loving, gentle, and have self-control, faith, peace, and joy (Galatians 5:22). As we exemplify the fruits of the spirit, it is the Comforter (Holy Spirit) being activated in our lives (John 14:26). What is impossible with man is possible with God (Luke 18:27)! We can overcome anything because we are more than conquerors! We can bear what the Father puts on us because He is with us helping us through! No good thing will (He) God keep from you (Psalm 84:11)!

Anyway, I started having second thoughts about this project. We get nervous sometimes don't we when we are not sure how the story ends? Or if we are not too sure about how it began? Will people like my book, my story, and appreciate my testimony? Everyone that sees your process will not appreciate it. Some will judge you based on your past, and say you have no chance for a future! You're too far gone! You are too messed up to think about writing a book. Your English is not good enough, or your content isn't strong enough!

But God gave me the confidence to keep my back straight to type. He kept my fingers loose enough to type! He would not allow me to stop but I heard in a still whisper, "go on." Have you ever got an assignment from God and as you are doing it, you think to quit? I remember saying, "LORD, this feels like soooooo many things are happening at once in my life. Am I starting over again?" Do you feel that way when it is time for you to elevate?

Sometimes we get tired of taking a class and doing the test. At times we all wish we could just learn the material without having to take the test to prove our knowledge. "I've just turned 60… LORD, I don't want to fight no more." Funny, because when I was in the world, I would have fought in a heartbeat, but now, this is different. LORD, I really don't feel like writing right about now. But Family, I have to say this; The LORD has been too good to me to stop here! He's just treated me absolutely marvelous. He's directed my heart & mind to just get this done!

So here I am to serve as a witness that God's

process doesn't stop when you get 60. It doesn't stop when you turn 40, it stops when you look like Christ. It stops when He finishes the work He started in you (2 Corinthians 8:11). He said to me, "I gave you the assignment to write about trusting my process, instead of the other jewels that I placed inside of you, son." (That's what He calls me, son.) As I heard Him talk more, He said, "There's no room & you don't have time to figure out, what I already have for you to do & to say.

Son, you don't need time to put anything together, because I've done the work for you. I'm directing your heart and your mind to all that's before you. "TRUST MY PROCESS"... He says, you don't need to experiment, to see what'll work, the best route to take, calculate a time frame, or anything... "TRUST MY PROCESS"!!!

There are some of us doing stuff right now we have never done. Starting businesses, raising children, thinking of dating again, getting married, dealing with the loss of our parents, friends, or other family members. Life is constantly changing, and all life's changes are part of your journey and God's process.

God is great at turning everything you go through to work to your good (Romans 8:28)! Be encouraged as you do something new! Writing this book is new for me! Starting a new job is new for me! Sharing my story in a public way is new for me!

But I must confess to have the confidence to trust God as you go through His Process, you must love Him! I mean really love Him, not sort of like Him, care about Him when things are convenient. You have to make your election sure that you are completely head over hills, sold out, ain't going nowhere like 4 flat tires love Him. Just down for God, because this love, will help you to Trust God's Process As You Go Through! Another something-something I wrote:

Original journal entry, entitled "Love"

Wow!!! This has taken me a few days to start on and I'm truly not sure if I'm actually at the point of expressing what's inside of me.

I do know that "Love is known only from the actions it exhibits!" That in itself sort of frightens me… I mean, what is love actually to me.

I love, I'm in love, I have loved, I want to love, I think I'm in love, and if not Lord, help me to love. I'm a man that has always had so many feelings in my heart for people. These past few days have me re-evaluating myself. Rather thinking, is it actually 'love' or am I 'highly emotional'?

I've been silent for five days as I ponder. I had to really pray & think about this… I was thinking defining love seemed easy enough to do, but I WAS FOOLED!!! It is a lot & I don't know if I'm able to express this concept briefly.

Love for me is being able to be totally vulnerable, honest, and putting everything on the table, with no inhibitions… and no holds bar. For now, love allows me to be able to receive unpleasantries, injury, pain, and hurt. If that's the case, I've experienced that a few times. But love for me is also being able to receive as well as help someone with being honest, broken, able to receive healing, mending, deliverance, or gain clarity of heart and mind.

Love is not being apathetic, but empathetic and sympathetic to someone's situation. This compassion allows me to be mindful of my own emotions, and how I can help the next soul.

Before I knew The Lord, I thought, imagined love was just what old people felt. I mean, I believed that you had to have lived 55-100yrs to really understand what it is. I thought many 'trials & errors' had to take place, then after all of that, if you were fortunate enough to have had 'battled the storm' and win, you were in an experienced condition to say that "love is this or that".

Instead, I found out this statement was the furthest from the truth. Yeah, I honestly thought of "love" as the ultimate goal in a marriage, in your career, and for your life to have meaning!! I understood family and friend love. We all had a best friend we grew up with that we shared everything with (Daryle aka 'Dannyboy'). All our secrets, all our plans when 'we grew up' we would share with each other.

I thought love had to do with your spouse, your children, your parents, and your prized possessions as I grew older. But my understanding of romantic love was limited. A long time ago, I would have told you, that love was "just a feeling". That the way folks knew they were in love was because they get a feeling in their stomach, butterflies, or something.

But that's not so!!! This is what "love" is truly to me now, and has been for some years...

God is love (1Jn 4:8)... That's so good, but "how much of God's love is really being displayed in me?" I've not been mean, nasty, cruel, or mistreated anyone, but is that enough? I'm in love with Jesus and I know because I see my fruit. I spend time with Him. I pray and talk with Him. I can laugh with Him and I walk every day with Him. It is my pursuit of Him that shows me what I truly love. I'm in love with my wife, I truly love my family, and I truly love my brethren. I pursue them and I try to demonstrate kindness, patience, faith, joy, self-control, and other fruits of the spirit.

I had to be sure that I wasn't in love with myself but in love with God and the things of God. Am I growing to love the 'lost'?? As I said in the beginning, "Love is known by what it exhibits!!" From my heart, am I exhibiting love?? How do I wanna exhibit love?

By living out the fruit of the spirit within my family, on my job, in my church, in my house also in my community. When we show others God through how we treat people, we are being the greatest ambassador for love one can be! The best evangelism tool to win souls for the Kingdom of God is living out the fruit of the spirit demonstrating love through exhibited actions.

Garry Washington

We are down to the wire now, for it comes down

to either we "TRUST GOD" or not… Now, in this process, at this time in eternity, with all that's going on on the earth, we're deep in the last days. The LORD is coming, there's no time to play games, or relax, but we should strongly consider catching up if we have fallen asleep!

Catch-up on what? Whatever you have to do to follow 'the process' of God. We get stuck in life when we stop following God. When we stop following Him, we lose our way and fall out of His will. If you want to get back to living and fulfilling your purpose, go back to the last instruction you got and follow it.

You stay intuned through prayer and following the direction of the Holy Spirit. Allow yourself to develop a true friendship with JESUS HIMSELF. Allow yourself to come to know who He is. Second, allow Him to direct you to the folks that have the same heart & are continually seeking The LORD also to keep you encouraged and motivated for your process.

Third, stay consistent even if you fail or have failed. I will tell you, I'm like King David, a man after God's own heart' (1SAM 13:14). Every day as often as you find in your day to do so, have a conversation with God. It doesn't have to be long & drawn-out, you can say "DADDY, I just want to tell you how much I love you and that I trust you.

Thank you for taking me through this process and not leaving me. I invite you to have your way in my life and help me to accept your direction. I love you God and again I tell you thank you and bless your holy name!"

For the Non-believers

For non-believers, please allow me to say if you do not have a relationship with DADDY… Please develop one!!! I know there are people out here saying they are Christians', but have no fruit to prove that. They are living lifestyles that are contrary to Biblical truth and too many don't see a problem with it. But do know that is a problem. I also know there is an audience that doesn't want to get to know God because of issues they have seen in the church.

I have heard many say they don't want to go to church because thieves, phony people, crooked pastors, or whatever are in the church. I am not here to defend the folks doing wrong, but I want to let you know, that God can reach you inside or outside the church. Where you meet God is between you and God, but get to know Him. Paul met Jesus on the Damascus Road. I heard the voice of God sitting at a kitchen table twice before I got saved. The location is not the issue, but your heart.

First, know that EVERYONE is imperfect. These folks that The LORD allowed to represent Him, all are imperfect too. We all make mistakes that are short of the glory of God. The Holy Script brings out in Rom 3:23 "For all have sinned, and come short of the glory of God".

Now family, PLEASE don't believe that I'm with the foolishness of those that are in positions of leadership doing wrong habitually without a concern. I am also not talking about people who choose to live in sin without remorse. There are believers out here battling sin and some may feel like they are losing it–but God!

Man will disappoint you every time and give up on you. But JESUS will NEVER disappoint you and he will never leave you nor forsake you when you are His!! Look, Imma tell you plain & simple, the world is dying and THE LORD IS ON HIS WAY!!! This world is on its way out. I would love for you to believe me, I truly pray for you to hear my plea and the pleas of God. It is not God's will that any man will perish but all will have everlasting life (2 Peter 3:8).

I encourage you to do as Psalms 34:8 says, "O taste and see that the LORD is good: blessed is the man that trusteth in Him". Family, I'm a living witness of "Gods' Grace & Mercies" upon a sinner headed for hell. I don't know how else to say it… There's no 'fantastic' way to say hell is real, it's hot, and if you don't accept Jesus as your Lord and Savior you cannot gain entry into His Kingdom.

Heaven and earth belong to God, and to get admission into the new heaven and earth, you must be born of His Spirit! You must become a kingdom citizen, and commit your life to His will for your life. This is not a light choice but a necessary one. This is no 'psyched-out' jargon, no 'hocus-pocus', 'wish-upon-a-star' foolishness. I'm gonna tell you the way it is & through 'The Grace Of God', His loving kindness touches your heart that you will want to see for yourself His love and grace.

"God is good, all the time & all the time, God

is good" we would always say growing up with the Big Mamas.

I truly encourage each of you to take a moment, find a space & ask The LORD for His direction in helping you to know Him. WHEW!!! I'm sitting here with my eyes watery, my heart is too full of compassion for each of you… I so want you to come to at least call on the name of JESUS, that you may know Him for yourself.

No matter WHAT is going on in your life now. How your life is looking right now. Or what you have been through or going through, don't miss God! The Lord is saying to you, RIGHT NOW, "Come unto me, all ye that labor and are heavy laden, and I will give you rest" (Matt 11:28).

If you want to rededicate your life or give your life to Christ, please understand the following. I don't want you to just say a prayer, I want you to pursue God. Read your Bible, pray, and seek His face (commandments, ways, and instructions about how to live).

Seek out the Holy Spirit and allow yourself to be filled. This isn't about religion but a connection to God the Father through His Son Jesus the Christ and His Spirit, the Holy Ghost! Let's start here with a Salvation prayer:

"Lord Jesus, I confess my sins (list: lying, stealing, cheating, fornication, adultery, whatever it is, do list them out) and ask for forgiveness. Father, I thank you for forgiving me of my sins and I pray that you show me how to do better and not repeat my mistakes. Father separate my old thoughts from my renewed mind. God, please renew my mind so that I think more like you and less like how I used to."

"Please send your Holy Spirit to dwell inside my heart, body, and mind. Father, I accept that Jesus Christ is your Son and that He is the only way to access You! That He lived, died, rose from the grave, and is seated next to you in heaven. Father on this day I call Jesus my Lord and Savior."

"From this day forward He is my Master and Teacher. Take complete control of my life and help me to walk in Your footsteps daily by the power of the Holy Spirit God. Help me to have the heart to read your Word and remember the things I read. Also, give me understanding Father of my purpose and Your will for my life. Thank you, Lord, for saving me and for answering my prayer. In Jesus name, Amen."

May our LORD & Savior, JESUS CHRIST become your Lord, your God, your Savior, your Friend.

Love You 2 Life

Garry Washington

Garry Washington was born December 7th, 1961 in Brooklyn, New York to his parents Darthus and Hellen. Garry is currently an active elder with his church who enjoys spending quiet time with God. He is passionate about giving back to the community, being a walking example, and demonstrating the love of Christ. Garry is happily married to Shirley (Shirl), has one daughter Shanice who he loves, and resides in Baltimore. He plans to write more books in the near future with the same heart–to please God and encourage His children.

Garry believes that no one is too far for God to touch their life. He wants to be a mouthpiece telling the nations about how good God has been to Him. Jesus is his Lord and Savior and he celebrates the day that God changed his life and turned his life around. Garry has experienced death, been to the morgue, and has walked out! He knows the power of God and how He is still working miracles in this life.

To learn more about Garry or to request him to speak, please visit GarryWashington.com or GWSpeaks.com or email: garry@klepub.com.

YOU Have a STORY

Have you been inspired by an Author?

YOU have **A Story**! What's **YOURS**?

KLE Publishing specializes in helping people become authors. In as little as 90 days, we can help you develop your book and publish to 39,000 outlets!

We help **YOU** Structure, Edit, Format
And can even write it for **YOU!**

Finance options available. No Credit Check or Minimum Score required to quaify.

770-240-0089 Ext 1

KLEPub.com Store

www.ingramcontent.com/pod-product-compliance
Lightning Source LLC
Chambersburg PA
CBHW072027110526
44592CB00012B/1418